What people are sayinc
always right; and 7.5 Oth ... yths Which Are Destroying Your Beauty Salon Business

"Power by name, power by nature. Ryan really knows his stuff and has helped me to double my business in the last two years. We have been open for almost seven years now, but only seen huge success more recently – all thanks to Hollie and Ryan at Salonology. The High Brow Beauty Bar has some big goals ahead to be achieved in the near future, and I can't wait to see where this takes us next."

– Katy, The High Brow Beauty Bar

"I cannot believe the difference joining Salonology Gold Club two years ago has made to both my business and me, as a person. I didn't learn marketing at college, but Ryan has taught me all the basics and more, helping my business flourish and my confidence soar. He teaches in an easy-to-understand format that anyone could put into practice straight away. Looking forward to the second book."

– Natalie, NM Beauty

"Since implementing the tips that Ryan has taught me over the last few years, I have been able to fall back in love with my business again. I've been able to find the perfect work-life balance and now enjoy working with high-value clients who appreciate my skills and are happy to pay for the privilege. You've truly given me back my spark and passion for my business."

– Sarah, Sarah Johnson Facialist

"The only industry book I ever read in full... and in only two days! Ryan just gets it, and doesn't make it boring. I couldn't put it down!"

– Nikki, Utopia Beauty Salon

"Fuss free, to-the-point information that's easy to follow and tailor to your business. An enjoyable read with a bit of humour thrown in for extra measure."

– Clare, Silhouette Skincare and Beauty Centre

There is business coaching and then there is Ryan Power and Salonology. Ryan's advice, inspiration, cheerleading and genuine awesomeness are all you need to help your business succeed. No bullshit, just super powers in marketing and common sense."

– Clare, The Nail Club

"Ryan is like the business partner I've always dreamed of! He's given me the tools, skills (and self-belief) to move my business forward from an expensive hobby to a business that now allows me to live my life on my terms. Can't wait for book number two!"

– Kerry, Body Sense Beauty Salon

"Ryan, Hollie and the Gold Club squad are my silent partners in my business. I am currently making new leaps into a bigger salon... I wouldn't have had the balls on my own! Thank you to you all!"

– Claire, Healing Flow Clinic

"We all thought we were stuck in a giant hole when Covid hit. We needed help. This book and the help from Ryan and Hollie got me and my business back on track. Definitely made me come out of my comfort zone. In my business and in life. Never give up!"

– Andrea, The Hair Branch

"I really loved Ryan's book! He has a great way of explaining things without using complicated jargon, and his positive energy is infectious. I learned so much from it and found it super useful. I highly recommend it to all salon owners who want to boss their marketing."

– Michelle, Perfection Skin and Beauty Clinic

THE **SUCCESSFUL** SALON MARKETING SYSTEM

How To Fill Your Beauty Salon Diary with Loyal and Happy Clients (Without Spending Thousands on Expensive Advertising)

RYAN POWER

ISBN 978-1-9162472-1-5
Published by Power Squared Publishing 2023

This one's for you, Chief.
You kept asking me when it would be finished; now it is.
I'll see you again when I get up there – for some long-overdue golf.

Contents

Preface 9

Introduction 15

Chapter 1 – THE STORY OF THE SALE 21

Chapter 2 – THE DISCOUNT-VOUCHER-SITE DISASTER 27

Chapter 3 – THE PRICE IS RIGHT 32

Chapter 4 – THE THREE WAYS TO GROW YOUR BUSINESS 41

Chapter 5 – LIMITED-EDITION UNIQUE EXPERIENCES 45

Chapter 6 – EMAIL: AN UNEXPECTED SECRET SAUCE 57

Chapter 7 – RUNNING COMPETITIONS THAT ACTUALLY WORK 70

Chapter 8 – DOMINATING FACEBOOK 81

Chapter 9 – RUNNING ADS 106

Chapter 10 – FEEDING YOUR SYSTEM 116

Chapter 11 – MARKETING 101 122

Chapter 12 – THE KNOW, LIKE AND TRUST FACTORS 132

Chapter 13 – THE PROFIT MAXIMISERS 143

Chapter 14 – WHAT WILL YOUR SYSTEM LOOK LIKE? 151

Your Next Steps 158

References 160

About the Author 162

PREFACE

When writing this book, I had a clear aim: create a replicable system that any salon owner can inject into their business to see an improvement in their results.

In fact, this system will work for you whether your business is a huge salon or you're a solopreneur, whether you've got a team of 20 or two, and regardless of where you sit on the wide spectrum of businesses which serve within our industry.

It matters not if you're a mobile hairdresser, owner of a high-street chain of brow bars, a reiki master based in your garden cabin, a lash artist operating from a spare bedroom at home or owner of a high-end day spa. If you apply the ideas and principles contained within these pages, then this will work for you.

When you integrate the Ultimate Salon Marketing System (or, for simplicity, just 'the System' from here on) into your business, you can look forward to not only greeting more new clients than you can handle but also seeing your existing clients returning far more frequently.

You'll also find it straightforward to market your business and easier to create content for your social media, and – should you wish – you'll finally be able to take a step back from your business, as some of your precious time will be gifted back to you from the System.

However, there is a caveat to all of this: none of it will work if you don't.

Getting a copy of this book is a wonderful start – and I both applaud and thank you for that – however, this is just the start.

I've heard it said that only a very small percentage of books that are started to be read actually get finished. So with that in mind, I wanted to give you a huge amount of value right up front. So much, in fact, that, if you don't read any more than just this introduction, you'll still more than have got your money's worth.

Does that sound fair? Great, then let's begin.

I will be sharing with you many of the strategies, tactics and, heck, let's even call them 'secrets to our success' in these pages. That's the success that led us to have a wonderful business, which delivered us a wonderful lifestyle and, ultimately, a wonderful payoff too.

All of these strategies that I'm going to share with you in this book absolutely do work. They worked for us, they've worked for many of the members of our paid-membership communities, and they can work for you too – if you put the graft in.

Now, I know that sounds kind of obvious. However, I really want it to sink in. Why do most people not have the success they truly crave?

Well, it's because they don't follow through with enough of the good ideas. Anyone can have a good idea; good ideas are not difficult to come by. You're going to get lots of them throughout this book.

In fact, you've probably had lots of good ideas before. Maybe some this week; maybe even some already today. The question is this: are you going to follow through with them? You see, the main problem is not ideas, but rather it's the implementation of them. That is where the magic happens. It's when you take what you learn and you put it into place in your business. This might be the most simple success strategy you will ever hear.

Now, here's an important side note. Whilst that is simple, it doesn't necessarily mean it's easy – because if it were easy to take action on all of your good ideas, then everyone would be doing it, everyone would be super successful and everyone would be driving around in their own obnoxious, fluorescent-green Lamborghini.

Sadly, we all understand that not everyone is super successful. In fact, a tiny percentage of businesses actually deliver the owner of the business the life of their dreams. I want you to be in that tiny minority.

I want you to have the life that you desire, whatever that looks like to you. Maybe you want to finish work at 2pm every day so that you can pick the kids up from school. Maybe you don't want to work at weekends. Maybe you only want to work two days per week, like Hollie did just before we sold our own salon and day spa.

Success looks different to different people. Whilst that's wonderful, you need to have an idea of what success looks like to *you*. Otherwise, how are you going to know whether or not you have achieved it?

If I could offer you one golden key to success, then this would be it: take action.

Taking determined, positive action every day – whether you feel like it or not – will be one of the main contributing factors to your success. The people who are typically the most successful are those who act, and who act with regularity (even when they don't feel like it) and whilst the idea shines bright.

I am going to encourage you to try to also make that change. Indeed, if you take nothing else away from this book, then I want you to make sure you take that away. *Take action.* That's it; two small, simple words.

We often talk about the importance of working on your business and not working in your business. Indeed, if you sincerely want to grow your business to its full potential, and if you truly want to enjoy freedom within your business and all the trappings that come with that, then you need to work on your business consistently and not simply be one of its employees.

Setting aside chunks of time – daily, if possible – to do the things we're going to discuss in this very book can change your life if you do it with regularity over time.

Of course, this is nothing new. It is nothing exclusive to our industry either. This works for everyone. And that is the, *ahem*, beauty of it. Sorry.

You have probably already worked out that owning and running a successful business isn't a stroll in the park. This is why the vast majority of businesses fail – and most of them within the first 12 months. This is partly because business owners spend much of their time doing the wrong things.

More often than not, they find themselves doing all of the jobs and not running the business. I don't want you to fall into that same trap. The good news is that most of your competition will also be following the same protocols. This gives you an opportunity to win.

Where you are right now in your business – and in your life – is a result of the choices and decisions you have made up until this point. If you want some different results and different outcomes moving forwards, then you need to change some of the inputs.

You cannot simply do the same things that you've been doing all along and expect different results. You have to make some changes. I am going to give you all the ammunition that you need in these pages. What you choose to do with it is entirely up to you.

We grew our day spa and salon from nothing to something very special. Prior to its rebirth, it was an underused – and tired – conference room in the basement of a Bournemouth hotel. With Hollie's vision, drive and determination, it became a nine-treatment-room, two-lounge, multi-award-winning business that was one of the premier day spas in the area.

In addition to that, it also hit the magical sweet spot of returning both profits and freedom. As mentioned, Hollie was only working two days per week by the time we sold the business in early 2020. In the last six months, I didn't venture in once, choosing to work remotely. The business paid for dozens of foreign holidays, nice cars and the beautiful home that we live in.

To be crystal clear, I'm not saying any of this to try to impress you. Rather, it's so you understand that this is possible for you also. In fact, you probably have a head start on us. When Hollie opened the spa, we didn't have even one day's experience in the beauty industry between us. Not one.

Anyone can build a successful business, but very few do. It is not because of a lack of imagination, it is not due to a lack of determination and it is not due to a lack of good ideas.

It's often due to lacking the correct implementation of those ideas into the business.

Don't be like everybody else. Be different. Do the work. Put the required effort in.

Don't get caught up in the daily grind, but rather take action every single day on the things that will truly move your business forwards.

Then everything can change for you.

It did for us.

INTRODUCTION

This is essentially a book about marketing. It's a true story too. This book breaks down the many things that we did to successfully transform our day spa and salon from an empty conference room in a hotel basement to a multi-award-winning business that people flocked to excitedly.

You could say that it's part biographical, part instructional and (hopefully) part inspirational too.

I'm going to share within these pages the things we tried, the things that failed and the things that worked so well we continued to concentrate on them day in and day out.

The truth about growing a successful business is that there are many ways to do it. The methods discussed in this book are in no way exhaustive. They are just what worked for us. I shall also outline some of the things we would be continuing to do today if we still owned our day spa and salon.

As mentioned previously, we sold our business early in 2020, after more than a decade of ownership. At the time of sale, the business was thriving: it had nine treatment rooms, two lounges and a dozen staff; it had won lots of awards and accolades; and it was a business that largely ran without the need for our daily input at a shop-floor level.

Of course, it wasn't always like that.

For the first few years, Hollie was working six days a week and every hour she was sent. Show me an entrepreneur who doesn't instinctively do that when they launch a new business! However, that wasn't always in her plan, and she was keen to delegate responsibility to free up her own time as much as possible. Smart move.

Still, this approach only works when you're making a profit. This is why getting our marketing right was a huge part of making the entire System work. Your business needs money to run. That money comes from your clients. Good marketing delivers those clients to you.

Much of marketing is simply trial and error. You try something, it doesn't work quite as you'd hoped, and so you make a few changes and try again. You then rinse and repeat.

Just make sure you're giving enough time for something to work. As business owners, we can be so impatient, can't we? I'm the same; I want the results yesterday! Of course, it doesn't work like that. It could take six to eight weeks to get someone from first hearing of you to becoming a client in your salon. Or longer!

This is why I recommend that marketing is something you do all the time – and not just when you've got white space in your diary. It should be something you're committing some of your weekly schedule to every week. After all, you want clients every week, don't you? In which case, you need to be doing something to attract them every week too. And that something is called 'marketing'.

By the end of our time here together, you're going to have a much better grasp of how to do it, and my wish for you is that, with some practice, you'll get very good at it. The good news is that it's a learnable skill. Anyone can improve their marketing skills. That includes you.

It's worth noting at this point that very few things work the first time. That's just a fact of life. Things will take longer than you'd hoped and will probably cost you more too. So it's best you know that up front. Do not let that put you off trying new things.

We tried so many things that didn't work. With some of them, we'd invested tens of thousands of pounds in them before we realised that it wasn't going to fund our early retirement to Florida after all! We've purchased equipment we thought would be the next big thing. We've set up entire new businesses that we thought would solve problems for the industry. None of it worked, and our poor little dog Maverick has had his inheritance reduced significantly on many occasions!

But that doesn't matter. It's good to try new things, even if they don't work out as you'd planned. This is how we learn. It's important to take some calculated risks once in a while.

Marketing will get you so far, but there's more to growing your business than just great marketing ideas.

There, I said it.

Sure, marketing is one of the more exciting elements of business (in my opinion, anyway, but then I am a fully grown man who still enjoys playing with Lego). However, there are lots of other working parts that make the System run smoothly. I will not be discussing those within these pages.

There will be no chapter on managing your team. No mention of recruitment, staff morale or team building. Nothing on choosing which treatments to offer or what area of the industry to specialise in.

That's not because those aren't important things – and certainly not because they didn't contribute to our success – rather, it's because they aren't my bag. I'm a marketing guy, and this is a marketing book.

I can help you with your marketing. I can get people queuing up outside your door. I can fill your diaries. That was my role within our day spa and salon, and that's my role here.

My amazing wife Hollie had already done most of the groundwork for our business long before I was on the scene. She'd already turned nothing into something. Her vision was already coming to life. She was already turning a healthy profit.

For the first four or five years, I had little involvement as I was running a totally different business altogether. However, when I sold that business, we both realised that many of the marketing strategies I'd learned would almost certainly work just as well for the salon industry as they had in my jewellery business. We were right.

My role was simple: to help make the salon even more profitable.

That's my goal for you too.

There's a good chance that you also already have a business. Perhaps one that is already making you a profit. Maybe you also just need a few tweaks here and there to turn something good into something great.

That's often all it takes: one or two good ideas, which – when implemented properly and executed consistently – can take you on to the next level. We've seen it with our own coaching clients time and time again.

You're going to discover many things that will work for you in the pages ahead. Don't leave the ideas in the book. Bring them to life in your own business. Put your own twist on them. Develop them further. Have some fun with them.

There are hundreds of ways to build up a profitable salon, and everyone does it slightly differently. Your mission is to find the one that works for you – and to take action on it.

Let's begin...

How to get the most from this book

I know, I know: you've read books before. I don't want to insult your intelligence here, but I do want you to get the maximum return on the investment from your time and effort in reading these pages.

I would absolutely encourage you to have a fresh notepad by your side as you start to go through this book, so you can scribble down anything that comes to you.

You will have lots of ideas about how this can work for you, and I don't want you to miss any of those. It's important to capture these ideas before they vanish again into the unknown.

I'll add a handy little summary of the main takeaways at the end of each chapter for you – including something to definitely model and something to absolutely avoid – and I'd again encourage you to stop in between chapters to mull over how this will look in your business.

Your version of the System will look a little different to how ours did by the end.

To make following along even easier, I've created this little visual, which I'll be revealing as the book goes on. No reading ahead now! All will be revealed in due course.

You'll discover what TC means in Chapter 8.

EB will be unveiled in Chapter 7.

KLTFs are in Chapter 12.

LEUE will be unmasked in Chapter 5.

Finally, PM will be brought to light in Chapter 13.

For now, I'll just flat-out tease you with this version of it:

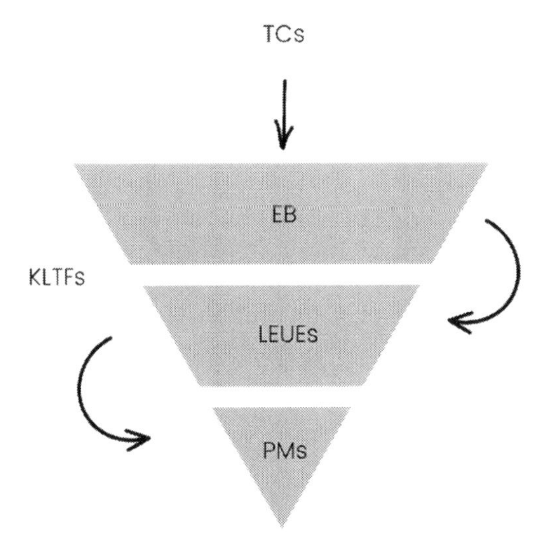

The Ultimate Salon Marketing System (the System)

Helpful, huh?

Trust me, it'll be worth the wait and all make perfect sense in due course.

Now, let's begin...

CHAPTER 1

THE STORY OF THE SALE

It was a warm and sunny Florida afternoon in Storey Lake, and Hollie and I were being shown around a stunning, waterside Orlando property.

Then the call came.

It was the solicitor back in England. The sale had gone through. We were no longer salon owners. After more than a decade of ownership, there was now someone new at the helm, and we could concentrate on helping others through our coaching business.

It was bitter sweet.

All of the ups and downs. The good times and the not-so-good ones. You know how it is on the entrepreneurial roller coaster, I know you do – however long you've been in business.

We took a moment to reflect on how far we'd come: from a figment of Hollie's imagination to something truly wonderful; and from one empty conference room in a hotel to nine treatment rooms, a dozen staff and thousands of happy clients. We had clients who returned regularly too – but we'll come to that in due course.

All of this with no real industry experience. Hollie wasn't even beauty qualified on the day we opened. When I came into the business, I'd barely set foot in a salon all of my life.

In retrospect, this may even have been an advantage. It meant that we had to employ staff on day one. It meant that we didn't have old industry habits holding us back. It meant that we questioned how everything was done to try to find better ways to do them.

It wasn't all smooth sailing, though. We had more than our fair share of downs as well as ups. It's par for the course with business ownership – not that you're warned about that before you take the plunge.

Just like many others, we experienced staff betrayals, unimaginable weather-based disasters, unfair customer reviews, months when we didn't know if we'd be able to pay our mortgage and times when we simply wanted to throw in the towel. Everyone has these.

It was during one of these periods of darkness that we knew we had to start doing something different.

It was sometime around 2012, and things weren't going so well. The salon was quieter than it needed to be, and we were starting to get a little concerned. We weren't quite at the stage of blind panic just yet, but that was the path we were heading along.

We were short on ideas, short on inspiration and even shorter on money. We needed some help, so we enrolled ourselves into a business-building seminar in Central London.

It was at a swanky hotel – the type where the door is opened for you by a chap in a top hat and white gloves – and it was filled with hundreds of other business types.

We'd not been to an event like this before, and it kind of felt a little like some sort of secret society.

As we walked into the basement of the hotel, we scanned the room nervously. It was akin to being back at school on the first day of term – and we felt like the new kids who'd arrived from a neighbouring school.

We had time to grab ourselves a much-needed cup of coffee before taking our seats in the main conference room.

What transpired over the next few hours really lit a fire underneath us. Sometimes, you only need one good idea to run with; however, we walked away with several to try. It was just the inspiration we needed.

The first real aha moment came for us early in the event. We heard three simple words, which have been ringing in my head ever since:

Success leaves clues.

It was so simple, but also bordering on the profound. It struck us like a thunderbolt. Here we were, trying to work everything out on our own, when there were already others who had it figured out.

We knew there were hundreds and hundreds of successful day spa owners out there; all we needed to do was mirror what they were doing and we'd be a sure-fire success. It was almost too easy. All we needed to do was find someone who'd share their secrets to success with us.

That part, it transpired, wasn't so easy. It turns out that not all successful business owners want to share how they did it. The spoilsports!

That aside, we were on to something. It's something that I don't want you to miss either.

Success – and also failure – leaves clues.

We often waste an extraordinary amount of time, resources and energy on trying to figure out how to do something when someone else has already figured it out.

Studying other businesses, watching how the successful salons operate, being around and sharing ideas with others who are a success, and modelling winning ideas are all wonderful shortcuts to where you want to go.

We were convinced that someone else must have built what we were looking for: a group of like-minded salon owners, all looking to grow their businesses with the help of someone who had been there and done it; a chance to share ideas and spur one another on; and a collective where everyone understands what the other group members are going through.

Sadly, at the time, that community didn't exist, so we were on our own (we've since built it ourselves, you may be pleased to know, and it's called the Salonology Gold Club).

The important lesson had been learned, however, and it's something we've applied ever since. You can learn from all of your own successes and failures, but you can also learn from those of other people too.

You can pick up the autobiographies of some of the most successful people who've ever lived and read their stories – successes and failures, warts and all – for less than the price of a decent mascara. That's something to consider.

Right then, though, we were about to embark on a journey of trial and error. We decided that we would try everything we could to see what worked and what didn't.

I committed to attending every seminar I could, to reading every book and to completing every online course I could get my greedy little trotters on. I didn't know where those golden keys would be, so the only thing I could think of was to explore everything.

Every month in the salon, we'd try something new. A new strategy. A new tactic. Something I'd learned, read about or even borrowed from another industry.

Sometimes, they worked, but more often, they didn't. You've most probably found that with the new stuff you've tried too.

We simply tried something new every month and then tested if it worked. If it did, then we'd keep doing it. If it didn't, then we'd drop it. That's a system I still use to this day, and one that you may wish to model for yourself.

Here's the other thing I learned: lots of things will work. There's more than one way to cook an egg, right? Who is to say which way is better than another? You need to find the ways that work for *you*.

The good news is that, in the pages that follow, I'm going to lay out an entire system that has been proven to work. All you need to do is implement it into your business.

Even then, however, there will be elements you'll want to tweak for your business, plus there is an almost endless number of ways to add new people into your version of the System. Perhaps you prefer the written word to recording videos. Perhaps you prefer Instagram to Facebook. Perhaps you love running open nights, but you cringe at the idea of networking.

The good news is that any and all of these can work. It's important for you to find what works for you, what resonates with your dream client (more on that later in Chapter 11) and what you actually enjoy doing. If you really dislike doing something, then it's hard to keep that up when the chips are down or when you're having an off day.

A phrase I picked up somewhere along the line – I think I heard it from Canadian motivational speaker Brian Tracy first – is that "There is no failure, only feedback."

When it goes right, we can learn from that.

When it doesn't, we can learn from that also. In fact, we learn much, much more from when it doesn't than from when it does.

Well, let's just say that the next thing we tried certainly provided us with a whole lot of this feedback – and it almost cost us our home too.

✓ **SOMETHING TO MODEL** – Success leaves clues. You don't have to figure everything out for yourself. Find others who have already achieved what you want and learn from them. It's a shortcut that can get you where you're going much faster and with less expense and/or stress.

✗ **SOMETHING TO AVOID** – Believing there's only one way to do anything. Take ideas and adapt them to suit your own life and business. Find your own best path.

CHAPTER 2

THE DISCOUNT-VOUCHER-SITE DISASTER

Understanding that, if we kept trying the same things over and over again, we were going to get more or less the same results, we knew that we needed to try some new ways to attract clients into our salon.

Everything in life is a series of inputs and outputs. Cause and effect. For each action there is an equal and opposite reaction (big up to Isaac Newton and his third law of motion).

If we wanted to get something different out (more clients, please), then we needed to put something different in (to switch up our marketing in some way).

We'd already tried lots of things at this point; some worked well, some worked not so well and some were an expensive disaster.

As mentioned before, much of marketing is testing. Even when you apply the strategies within these pages, you'll still want to test and tweak certain elements to fit you and your business. That's what it's about. When you find something that works, then you can double down on it; when something doesn't work, then you either tweak it or pull the plug.

Around the time we realised this, the online landscape looked very different. Facebook was in its infancy, and there was no Instagram or TikTok. Imagine that.

There was, however, a growing number of daily-voucher sites – and, boy, were they popular.

The premise of them was fairly simple: as an end user, you register on the website, and every day, it'll send you a whole host of offers it believes you'll love. All of these have a huge discount – sometimes as much as 80% or more. The end user buys the voucher from the website, and the website splits the money with the retailer.

All great, right?

Well, maybe in theory; it's certainly great for the client, but it's not always quite so great for the retailer.

First, the websites sell this premise to the retailer on the basis that you will take a hit on this first sale (and a very large one, potentially), but it's all good, as the customer will then keep coming back for years, and you'll make all of your money back.

This is kind of like the same principle that supermarkets apply, called 'loss leaders'. The idea is that, if you go into the supermarket and grab yourself some coffee with 50% off, there's every chance that, whilst you're there, you'll also get the rest of your weekly shopping, and thus the supermarket makes its money back.

Whilst that sounds great in theory, it's not without problems. You're going to need a good system in place to ensure that these clients come back and enjoy your wares again. If you're not doing a good job at this, then you're going to lose out.

Sadly, there's an even bigger problem. Think about the type of person who excitedly opens those voucher emails every morning, scanning the information for the cheapest deal they can find. What sort of person is that? Is that one you'd ideally like to use your business? Or would you prefer someone who is happy and willing to pay the full asking price?

These voucher sites attract bargain hunters. I don't need to tell you that you don't want those people flooding your business – not least because they are typically loyal to the voucher site and not the retailer. What a kick in the teeth!

You can do an amazing job of looking after them – taking a huge financial hit in the process, remember – and then, after all of that, they simply follow the voucher site to the place up the road that is running the next cheap deal.

It does make you wonder why anyone in our industry would agree to doing these in the first place, doesn't it?

Well, here's the reason: incredibly persuasive and borderline-aggressive telesales staff.

We had the call. Did we want to run a 'special promotion' for our salon?

Of course, knowing what we know now, there's no way that we would have even entertained this idea. But you only know what you know – and this was an exciting new opportunity at the time. Not everyone was doing them, and we knew that it would get us in front of a lot of people. Not the right people, we later discovered, but people all the same.

Fortunately for them, they had also called at an opportune moment. We needed the business. The telephone representative worked on us hard, and we agreed to what, looking back, was a crazy deal.

The next part, we simply weren't prepared for.

Now this was back in the day when the voucher sites were just beginning. They were incredibly popular, and the way they sold the deals was that there was no maximum number of sales and the voucher was only on sale for 24 hours. You had to get it that day or you missed out. This meant that their websites were visited regularly, and their daily emails were opened with rabid anticipation by their bargain-hunting masses.

It turned out that our deal sold well. Like, really well. As in, 'more than 800 people claimed the offer in 24 hours' kind of well.

Brilliant, right?

Well, not so much. We were losing big time on each and every one of these vouchers, and it soon got worse. The clients were certainly not our target demographic. Many were rude, and they all wanted something for nothing. Most of them never came back – although that was a blessing in many ways.

To top it all off, we had to pay the voucher site their 50% of the takings too – plus VAT on top.

After we'd paid our team, we were losing money on every single voucher redeemed. All 810 of them.

There were times immediately after this that we wondered if we'd even make it through. There was just no money left in the business, and this was during a time when we were already looking at new ways to make money, not lose more of it!

Since then, I've cringed every time I see a salon – or any service business – run deals on these kinds of sites. I'm not saying they can't work for anyone, but from all the salon owners I've ever spoken to about their experiences – and there's a lot of those – then the experience is an expensive one for more than 90% of them.

We did, however, learn lots of really important lessons from this experience.

The first was about pricing yourself correctly...

✓ **SOMETHING TO MODEL** – Everything output has an input. If you want to change some of the outputs in your business, then you need to trace them back to the input and change that.

✗ **SOMETHING TO AVOID** – Making impulsive decisions based on persuasive sales reps. Do your due diligence, do your research and really think through your big business decisions before you leap.

CHAPTER 3

THE PRICE IS RIGHT

Let's talk about pricing.

I imagine some of you will be aghast just at the mere mention of that word. The same readers will probably know that, deep down, they haven't priced themselves correctly.

You'll know if that's you because you won't be making as much profit as you'd like.

Whilst I did cover this topic in my first book, it's so damned important – now more than ever, in fact – that I'm going to dive in again. It's also essential to have this nailed down if you're going to implement the System into your business.

In addition, I see first-hand every week salons that are not only not charging their worth but that are, quite frankly, winging it with a pricing structure plucked out of thin air.

Thankfully, I've got your back.

Here's how many service-led businesses – and not only those in the salon world, to be fair – price themselves:

Step one – See what other people are charging for the same service.

Step two – Take an average of these prices.

Step three – Reduce that number by 10–20% to ensure they are 'competitive'.

Step four – Panic when competitors lower their prices, realising they are in a race to the bottom of the market.

Step five – Forever face an uphill battle of exchanging time for money and, quite frankly, not having enough of either.

Step six – Throw in the towel in favour of taking an employed role, whilst complaining it's impossible to make any money in this industry.

Now I don't know if any of that sounds familiar or not, but allow me to explain first why this is so flawed, as well as offer you a better strategy. Don't worry, I won't call you out if you've adopted this within your business; the reason I bring it up is because so many people do just this and are effectively dead in the water right from the get-go. There's no need to be harsh on yourself or beat yourself up about it, but there's every need to make the changes needed – and, quite possibly, yesterday.

The first huge issue with all of this is step one. You know all those other people whose pricing you were basing yours on? Yeah, they probably aren't making any money. Very few business owners really are. Most are just about getting by, if that. And I know that wasn't what you had in mind when you decided to start your business, was it?

In 2020 – and this was before the Covid pandemic – the average small-to-medium-sized business in the UK made a profit of just £8,000 per year.[1] That's just over £150 per week. I can only imagine those numbers have dropped since too.

So, right away, we have an issue here. We're basing everything on a business or businesses that we know next to nothing about. Even if they are making a profit, then we don't know how much or on which services or treatments. We also have no idea about the costs of these businesses, the hopes and dreams of their owners, whether the owners pay themselves a salary or not, or any number of other key metrics.

This is going to get worse before it gets better too.

Let's assume you've gone ahead and priced yourself in the way laid out previously. What happens when new competition enters the market? Our industry has very low barriers to entry, and it's not uncommon for competition to just spring up, right on your doorstep and seemingly overnight.

Let's also assume that said new competition has also decided to calculate – and I use that word very loosely indeed – their prices in this manner. Their prices are therefore going to be lower than yours. You'll no doubt be itching to drop yours even further to keep in line with this. This will happen every time another competitor enters the market. It's a never-ending spiral to the bottom. It's not fun, and it's highly unlikely to be profitable for you.

Chances are that there will be lots of businesses all fighting over the same scraps. What compounds how ridiculous this whole scenario is are those you're all battling over. When I say 'scraps', I mean that. It's the wrong end of the market.

It's those clients I described at the end of the last chapter who jumped all over our voucher deal. Those who want something for nothing. Those who complain at the smallest thing in the hope of a free treatment next time or some money back. Those who don't buy the products you recommend. Those who write unfair reviews online. Those who then leave when they find a less expensive alternative elsewhere.

They probably are not what one would describe as your dream target client (we'll come to working out who they are – and how to find them – later in the book in Chapter 11).

Now I understand you may still be sceptical at this point. After all, we all want the cheapest version of everything, right? Well, let's take a moment to explore that idea.

Many do indeed believe that people make purchase decisions based on price. And some do. Mostly our friends who snapped up all of those voucher deals. Of course, we know what great clients they make.

There are some times when price *is* the key driving factor. However, this is typically only true for commodities (that is, a basic good that can be easily exchanged for another). The marketplace treats these the same, no matter who made them or who is delivering them. For example, nuts and bolts or screws. You're not going to pay a premium for these or care who made them. Is that the same for what you offer, though? I really hope not.

Let's take a look at a few other examples to drill this point home, shall we?

When you are hungry, is price the most important factor? If so, we'd all be eating value-label beans or noodles for 20p a meal, three times per day.

When you want to go from point A to point B, is price the key factor? If so, then nobody would buy a new car when you can pick up an old banger for £500. Or get a bike for even less. Or take the bus. Or just walk, which is free.

How about clothes? Who would shop at designer outlets when the charity shops and car boot sales offer such gloriously low prices.

The truth of the matter is that, when your clients are making a choice about where to take their business, they are taking far more into consideration than the pounds and pence alone. They are considering the value. The brand. The reputation. The experience. The status. They are influenced by cultural, social, personal and psychological factors.

It's not just about the money. At least, it isn't for the clients you actually want to serve.

Rather than battling it out at the lower end of the market, I'd encourage you to set your sights a little higher. When you target the upper end of the market, then lots of magical things take place.

First, you actually make more profit, which is nice, given it's essential for your very survival.

Second, you're going to attract a totally different type of client. One who actually appreciates you and is loyal to you. One who has the capacity and desire to take your product suggestions. One who recommends you and brings their friends along with them when they visit. Altogether, a type of client you'll love serving.

Third – and this is really key for a long-term relationship – you'll be able to really wow your clients. You'll have the money in your business to invest in the best products, which will ensure the best results for them. You'll have the funds to add all the little touches that people really appreciate and associate with premium service providers. You'll be able to pay a market-leading wage to attract the best staff. You'll be able to afford to market your business in a way that others simply can't.

All of this, and so much more, is available to you when you price for profit. And if all of that weren't enough, you'll also stand out from the crowd and have less competition, as everyone else is targeting those aforementioned scraps.

So, if you don't work out your pricing the way explained at the beginning of this chapter, how do you do it?

Well, the first golden rule of pricing is this: pricing is a mathematical decision and not an emotional one. I know we're in an emotion-driven industry, but you can't pay your bills with emotions. You simply have to work out your pricing in such a way that you'll know without fail that each and every treatment or service you deliver is making you a profit.

Are you making a profit on each of your services? Do you even know? Whilst ignorance can be bliss, you need to know this. I am sympathetic to the fact that probably not that many within our industry are keen mathematicians, so I'm going to break this down in the simplest way I can – as well as offering another solution immediately afterwards.

In order for your business to make a profit, you have to have more money coming in than going out. Your profit will be the figure that is left once all of the bills have been paid out of the money you've collected.

Hopefully, this sounds simple enough, and it is; so what's the problem? Well, one of the problems is all the hidden costs of running your business. I say 'hidden', but maybe 'forgotten' would be a better description.

It's easy to include the obvious things when we're talking about costs: rent, products, staff wages and the like.

However, how about some of the less obvious ones, such as insurance, business rates and a music licence? Who is paying for these? And what about those final costs, such as the slice for His Majesty's government or your own salary?

The bottom line is that, if you're not billing all of these costs to your clients – via the pricing of your treatments or services – then you'll be footing the bill. Or in a shocking number of cases, you'll not be able to take a proper salary for yourself. Probably not what you had in mind when drafting out that business plan at the start of your journey.

The purpose of any business is to make a profit for the owners or shareholders. Any business that doesn't generate any profit over the long term is either a charity or a very expensive hobby. And that's the truth.

So the goal is therefore to ensure that there is money left over once all of those bills have been paid, right? And I really do mean every bill – and especially the one you pay to yourself once all the others have been settled.

Here's how I like to think about it: every single treatment or service you deliver pays a little chunk towards those bills. Not just the costs that are directly proportional to the treatment, such as consumables and wages, but every cost. That means when you – or one of your team – carry out a massage, for example, then a tiny piece of the revenue that massage generates needs to go towards your rent. Another piece goes towards your broadband. Another still goes towards keeping the lights on. Yet another goes towards uniforms. And so on and so forth, until each and every bill is covered. Professional fees, stock, printing, booking software, website maintenance, telephone lines, decor, furniture, data storage and credit card processing fees – *everything!*

Can you now see why it's so important not only to have a solid grasp on what all of these costs are (and my previous list is far from exhaustive, by the way) but also why it's going to be really difficult – if not impossible – to have any sort of profit left over if you're charging peanuts for what you or your team are delivering? It should also help to demonstrate why guesswork isn't going to cut it.

It will be vital to you to completely understand all of your costs and how they relate to the prices you charge. Likewise, you should know how much it costs to keep the doors open, as well as your break-even point (the point at which the revenue you generate covers all costs).

If this all sounds like gobbledygook to you, then I'd suggest sitting down with your accountant and asking for some personal guidance. This is certainly an area where ignorance isn't bliss, and you should seek professional advice if you feel you need it.

(As a side note, if you're a member of our Salonology Gold Club, then you can use the simple calculator we've created, which does all of the heavy lifting for you. You'll find it in our private member's hub. Visit www.salonologygoldclub.com if you're not a member but want access to that tool.)

It's really important that you take the time to do this before moving on. Many of the concepts discussed in this book will not work if you're not priced for profit. Plus, who wants to work for free, anyway?

Don't put it off; do the work. Doing this exercise and pricing yourself correctly could be worth tens of thousands of pounds to you each year from this point forwards. From a return-on-investment standpoint, that's a wonderful use of an hour of your time, wouldn't you agree?

Put the book down and do it right now. Don't worry, I'll wait.

Following the voucher-site debacle, we learned our very expensive lesson and adjusted all of our prices accordingly. Many salon owners we work with are gobsmacked when they realise their actual level of profit for specific treatments (or as the case occasionally is, losses rather than profits).

In fact, we reviewed and raised our salon prices every year, which is something I'd recommend you do too. Your costs are going to increase every year, and every time they do, then the additional money to cover that is coming straight from your pockets – unless you charge them to your clients effectively.

This means that, every year you don't raise your prices, you become less profitable. You may feel that protecting your clients from this is admirable. It's not. I understand that you love your clients and you love helping them, but you also owe it to them to help them at the highest level you can – and that requires the very best of you. You need to feel appreciated. You need to feel as though you're making progress. You need to feel as though you're not working for free – because that doesn't bring out the best in anyone.

Remember, without a profit you just have a very expensive hobby

---

✓ SOMETHING TO MODEL – Do your numbers properly. Get help from someone if you're really struggling with the mathematics, and ensure that you make a profit with every service you deliver. Ignorance here is very expensive, and nobody wants to be working for free all of the time – no matter how much you love your job or your clients.

✘ SOMETHING TO AVOID – Getting into a price war. It's a flat-out race to the bottom and a terrible position to be in strategically for any business. You'll attract better clients – and actually be able to make a decent living – when you price yourself profitably and aim your services at people who appreciate you.

CHAPTER 4

THE THREE WAYS TO GROW YOUR BUSINESS

Sometimes, things happen in life that you have no explanation for. Sometimes, something terrible has to happen to make way for something even more incredible.

So it was for us.

We were still reeling from the financial clusterfuck caused by our little voucher-site episode.

Ironically, that was about to become one of the best things that ever happened to us. First, however, came a chance encounter with a marketing great, which opened my eyes wider than they'd ever been opened before.

I mentioned earlier in the book that, around this time, I was greedily devouring as much content as I possibly could in search of that elusive golden nugget. You never know where or when the inspiration will strike, but during another seminar I'd heard someone mention the work of American marketing great Jay Abraham.[i]

I immediately went to check him out, and one of his presentations really caught my interest, in which he spoke of there being only three ways to grow any business.[2]

---

[i] You can learn more about the teachings of Jay Abraham on his website: www.abraham.com

Yup, just three.

This immediately grabbed my attention, as I felt that I could list at least a dozen ways. I mean, there was email, social media, leaflet drops, radio advertising, magazines, newspapers and so much more.

However, it turns out that I didn't quite understand at that point.

I do now.

The first way to grow your business is to *attract more customers*. This is one that most business owners turn to by way of a knee-jerk reaction when things aren't quite going as they wanted.

The second way to grow your business is to *increase the frequency with which people do business with you*. That is, the same number of customers, but more transactions. This is going after the customers you already have and encouraging them to come back more often.

The third way to grow your business is to *increase the average spend per transaction*. Again, potentially, you have the same number of clients, but they are spending more money each time they are with you.

Most business owners I speak to are focusing predominantly on getting more clients in. Once I share this with them, their focus tends to change a little. Perhaps yours will too.

Here's the thing...

It costs six times as much money to attract a new client as it does to get an existing client to return.[3] Six times! Given your new appreciation for the relationship between costs and profit (from the last chapter), you also can hopefully see what a revelation this is!

You see, your existing clients know you, like you, trust you and, in some cases, even love you. So it's naturally going to be much, much more simple – and more cost-effective – to get these same people coming back more and more often.

It's also much easier to get your existing clients spending more money with you – as long as you give them plenty of good reasons to do so. What's the number one reason your clients aren't visiting you more or spending more money with you? You're probably not giving them a good-enough reason to.

This really had me excited – and the best part was yet to come.

If you manage to double (which is unlikely in itself, but stay with me) any of the three ways listed before, then you'll double your revenues.

Pretty cool.

Let's say you have 100 clients, they each spend an average of £50 every time they are with you, and they each visit you four times per year. Broadly speaking, your revenue will be this:

100 x £50 x 4 = £20,000

Double any one of those, and you'll double your business. That's not easy to do, but I just want to demonstrate the mathematics here for a moment:

200 x £50 x 4 = £40,000
or
100 x **£100** x 4 = £40,000
or
100 x £50 x **8** = £40,000

Whichever of the three 'levers' you pull, it impacts the end result in the same way.

But here comes the really interesting part: what happens when you pull all three levers at the same time?

The growth you can achieve is exponential and no longer linear. Increasing any one of the three levers by 10% will increase the overall revenue generated by the same 10%.

But what if you increase them all by 10%? Well, that hikes your revenue by 33%.

What if you increase them all by 33%? Bravo, partner, you've just doubled your business.

To think, there we were, constantly focusing our thoughts, efforts and attention on getting more clients. Maybe you are doing the same. When, really, the riches are to be found not only in attracting some new clients but also in getting them coming back more often and spending more each time they are with us.

How much time, effort and thought are you investing in getting your clients to return more frequently and, ideally, spend more money with you whilst in your company? Maybe you're not spending any. Many aren't. If you're not, then I've good news for you: you've got some serious untapped riches locked up in your business.

For now, though, I want us to concentrate on what Hollie came up with, so that you can potentially look forward to similar breathtaking results.

✓ **SOMETHING TO MODEL** – Don't just focus on getting new clients. Sure, they are important, but the faster routes to the success you desire are found in concentrating on your existing clients and serving them more regularly, at a higher level or both.

✘ **SOMETHING TO AVOID** – Thinking you already know it all. Attend seminars, read books, watch webinars and learn from others. You never know what will unlock the door for you.

CHAPTER 5

LIMITED-EDITION UNIQUE EXPERIENCES (LEUEs)

We were racking our collective brains.

What could we do that would attract new clients whilst also encouraging our existing ones to return more frequently and also spend more money at the same time?

It seemed like an impossible conundrum.

"What if the voucher sites were on to something?" Hollie asked casually, one morning. "Is there a way that we could somehow replicate the principles of what they were doing to attract people, but whilst remaining profitable ourselves? How can we give people a great reason to come back every month, if possible, and always spend when they return?"

She had picked up the scent and wasn't going to let it go.

At this point, I must add that I cannot claim credit for any of this part. This was all Hollie's wondrous idea.

After much brain dumping, brainstorming, and plenty of back and forth, we had a concept. It was something that, in turn, became the one thing we did that exploded our business more than any other. It was something that the rest of our team also got behind and contributed to.

Behold the monthly limited-edition unique experience (LEUE)!

We're in the experience industry. People will pay more for an experience – and they'll more readily tell their friends about them too.

A massage is great, but a 'de-stress and detoxify afternoon experience' with their friend is far better, more valuable in the eyes of the client and much easier to sell too.

One of the things so many struggle with – especially in today's competitive marketplace – is that others are offering what appear to be similar services and treatments at a fraction of the price. How does the client know that your manicure will be any better than the one being peddled down the road for £20 less?

When you offer a limited-edition experience, you're in a category of one. Nobody else is selling that. Heck, even you aren't selling it a month from now – but more on that later in this chapter.

If people take to Google to compare your experience with others, they won't be able to. You'll be dominating that little space, and when the number of options available goes down, then the price goes up as a result. That's basic economics right there.

So each and every month – for many, many years – Hollie and our team would come up with a unique monthly experience. The idea, remember, was to not only encourage new custom but also to give our existing customers a great reason to come back more regularly. You'd be amazed at how many people would gladly give you more money more frequently if only you gave them a good reason to. This was our good reason, and we did it every month.

The inspiration for each month often came from an event that was taking place or some form of seasonal variation. For example, in the summer, we may do a Wimbledon-themed experience, as the whole country would be talking tennis; in October, a Halloween-based experience might make sense; and in January, it could all be based around detoxifying after festive excesses!

The truth of the matter is that you can create a unique experience around pretty much anything. It becomes even easier when you wrap it around a good story. A good story gives you a simple way to market the experience to your customers without them getting bored. If I messaged you month after month about just a standard massage, then I'm going to run out of creativity pretty quickly, you'll lose interest, and I won't sell you anything.

If I can pique your interest with an interesting story about how and why we're doing this, then I can far more easily capture your attention month after month without you getting fed up. In fact, such was the success of this that, eventually, we had people climbing over one another for the spaces available and blindly booking before we even announced what some of the experiences were!

That was partly due to one of the most important elements of the LEUE: the limited bit.

One of the most powerful tools in the marketer's toolkit is scarcity. Tell people that they can have as many as they want of something, and it loses value. Tell people that you've only got one of something, and all of a sudden, the value goes up immensely. Just take a look at any number of luxury items, which are all made in very limited quantities. Handbags, shoes, very fast cars, paintings, yachts and mansions – you get the idea.

If just anyone could buy a Ferrari, then they would no longer be as desirable. It's the fact that everyone can't get one that makes everyone without one want one. It's all about the human psychology involved – and that's what's going to help you sell more of your experiences.

When speaking in terms of scarcity, we have two levers that we can pull. The first is quantity. This is us saying that we only have a limited number of these available. Again, this is very common in other industries, and it's a hugely persuasive tool. You're basically saying that you've got space for only four people, and when they're gone, they're gone. This taps into the fear of missing out (FOMO) which, again, is a real driver for making people take action. Starting to use this alone in your marketing will have a hugely positive impact on your business.

The second lever is time. This is us saying that you have to buy before the end of the month or it won't be available any more. It's very simple for clients to understand and is also incredibly persuasive. People often need a deadline to prompt them to take action. Remember, that's what we're trying to make them do: take action. If you say to someone that something is available for as long as they want, then where's the incentive for them to dive in and commit?

Our original plan was to get people coming in to see us more frequently than they were currently doing: ideally, every month. Our plan was simply to ensure that they missed out if they didn't take action.

Stick a deadline on it, and all of a sudden, people will be panicking as the date draws close. Expect lots and lots of sales as the deadline approaches, as well as people calling you after the date has passed, begging and pleading and claiming they didn't read any of the emails stating it was going away again.

Want to know what you can do to really maximise those sales and have your clients forming a less-than-orderly queue outside your door and climbing over one another to secure one of the limited spots?

Combine both scarcity in quantity and scarcity in time at once. This is saying to people that not only do you just have a certain number of slots available in your diary but, in addition to that, you're taking it away at the end of the month. This is the holy grail of using scarcity to drive custom.

Interestingly, we used the time factor every month (everything we did was for just one month only, so there were 12 LEUEs per year); however, we didn't always limit the number of spaces. That really depended on what was going on in the salon, how many staff hours were available that month, how busy the diaries already were and a number of other factors. The numbers changing each time also kept an element of intrigue, and it didn't look like we were simply rehashing the same thing every month (which, to be clear, we weren't).

A word of warning about scarcity: only harness its powers for good, not evil. What I mean by this is that it would be easy to say you've only got two spaces left, but then keep selling more. You see lots of internet types doing this. Fake countdowns and limited numbers that mean nothing – that sort of thing. Not only is this dishonest but it's also the highest form of marketing douchebaggery. Don't do it. If you have 10 spaces left, then say that. You'll be found out at some point, and you'll lose all integrity in the marketplace, followed by losing all of your clients. It's just not cool.

Since putting this into place in our business, I now see other companies doing this all the time. Now I've mentioned it, you'll notice it too. McDonalds' restaurants (and, boy, do I use the term 'restaurants' loosely) do it with regularity. You've seen the ads: "Grab your limited-edition Texas Rodeo burger for £1.99, but only until 3rd March when it goes away forever. Lasso one today whilst you can, partner!"

All McDonalds is doing is adding a different sauce to a burger it typically already offers, giving you a reason to go and buy one, before slapping a deadline on it. It's smart, and I've no doubt that it drives McDonalds' burger sales – especially during otherwise slow trading periods.

It isn't alone either. KFC and Burger King also do the same. So do all of the nationwide pizza delivery companies; have you ever noticed that the Dominos flyers you get through your door pretty much weekly always have a different promotion on? That's not a coincidence; that's by design. They want to give you reasons to buy, and if the first promotion didn't work, then, by Jove, they'll try another one.

Our experiences were always limited editions, and we also liked to use the term 'off menu'. Again, this drives intrigue and makes it much easier to attract attention from a marketing perspective.

We were typically giving one or more of the treatments we usually offered a special twist – which we didn't usually offer. We might then add in a few little quirks or extras to tie in with the theme or the story being told, and then we'd give it a unique name before making it available for that month only.

Now, here's the part where lots of people go wrong, and I don't want that to happen to you. I want you to pay special attention to the next part, okay?

This is not about discounting your services or treatments. I'll say that again: this is *not* about discounting your services or treatments. It wasn't *that* part of the voucher-site set-up that we were modelling here, and I don't recommend that you do either.

I really can't hammer this point home enough, as I know the temptation will be to make it as cheap as chips. So, one final time in both italics and bold type:

This is not about discounting your services or treatments.

To begin with, you don't need to. People get very excited about the thought of unique, off-menu experiences, so the experiences really do sell themselves when done correctly.

Second, we know what sort of customers are attracted to the '80% off this week' type offers. We simply don't want those people in our business. (Sorry, not sorry.)

Third, the idea, remember, was in part to increase the average client spend. Not having our girls working back to back delivering treatments that made us no money. We'd tried that already and had no intention of replicating that ever again!

So, it's imperative that your LEUEs are profitable.

I mean, I shouldn't have to say that, really, but having seen so many social media posts over the years from people representing our industry, I think I probably should. Go back and do your pricing again to ensure – without a shadow of a doubt – that you're priced for profit.

Ensuring that you're correctly priced means you're able to add value for your clients. Please understand the phraseology I've used: *add value*, don't discount. Discounting is simply slashing your prices. Adding value is incorporating additional items of value into your offer – ideally ones that don't cost you very much – which make the experience truly unique and capture the attention of your clients.

For example, discounting a massage would mean that you reduce the price for the month; for example, from £70 to £50. Adding value would mean that all massages that month get a luxury oil upgrade, plus a glass of fizz afterwards – together valued at £24 – without any additional charge.

One of those examples would sell much better than the other. The same one of them would make more money too, attract better clientele and have the clients talking about it afterwards.

Don't discount, add value.

World-famous investor Warren Buffett says, "Price is what you pay and value is what you get."

That's a saying worth remembering. You want to try to give your clients a bigger stack of value than what they are paying you for. That way, it's an easier buying decision for them to make, and they'll be delighted with their purchase. There is nothing worse than feeling short changed by someone, right? In business, as a whole, the easier we can make it for someone to do business with us, then the more likely they are to do so. This makes it easier for them to say yes, and that's what we want.

So, let's take a look at what this might actually look like in your business, shall we?

Now, of course, it depends very much on the products and services that you offer, as well as on your ability to be creative (although we do have a solution for that too, which is coming later in Chapter 15).

Typically, you'll be bundling up a number of the services or treatments that you offer, adding a unique twist of some sort to take it off menu, sprinkling some additional sparkle on top and, finally, giving it a catchy name.

Here are some examples to demonstrate:

> *'Strawberries and Cream Indulgence'*
>
> *To celebrate Wimbledon this June, enjoy our gorgeous 'strawberries and cream indulgence' treatment. Using a strawberry-infused body*

scrub, we will gently buff you from top to toe, leaving your skin fresh and glowing, before a warmed strawberry oil is drizzled over you to deeply moisturise your skin. Whilst cocooned in a fresh cotton wrap, we will massage your scalp, relaxing you deeply. To finish, a vanilla-scented body butter will be applied as we massage your body – absolute heaven.

Can you see how, with a few extra touches and a little glitter sprinkled on top, we've transformed this from just another massage to a truly unique experience (which, let's be honest, sounds amazing!)?

'Ready for Sundowners'

Feel your best during these summer months with our exclusive package. We'll have you feeling your absolute brightest, with a lash lift, brow shape with a tint, and our limited-edition lime-and-lemongrass manicure and pedicure. Join us with a friend to get a glass of fizz each too!

Again, this has been taken from a small package of glam treatments to become something with a unique twist. Here, we've encouraged (bribed!) them to bring a friend along for the ride too!

(As a side note, please don't offer alcoholic fizz unless you have a licence, and make sure you check the local laws in your area around this.)

'Melt Me Away!'

This September, we aim to bring back the energy after the summer and help you to maintain your glow from the warmer months. Using a truly divine caramel-scented oil to delight the senses, we start with a deeply relaxing Indian head massage, focusing on all those tension points, to send you into a deep state of relaxation. Then we move on to the face and carry out a luxurious facial suited to your skin type, focusing again on the facial massage and pressure points.

This is little more than a massage and a facial; however, the way it's wrapped up and sold makes all the difference.

Hopefully, you've got the idea of what we're looking to achieve here. Delicious combinations of treatments that sound just as divine as they truly are.

Again, I'm going to stress the importance of knowing your numbers. I know, I know, but it really is that important. In fact, it's essential to your business's survival.

Don't just make the numbers up because they sound good. Run them first. Make sure that you're making a profit (a good profit) on each and every offering you do.

There's no magical formula for this part, sadly. Ultimately, the monthly LEUEs that perform the best will depend on what you present, how you present it, the capacity of your business, your target market and plenty of other external factors too.

The best advice I can give you here is to test, test, test.

Try different stuff out and look for trends. If something sells like wildfire, then remember that and think about how you can do something similar – but with a slightly different twist – down the line. You don't need to reinvent the wheel every single time.

We tried some at £49, some at £79 and others well past £499. We tried some with places that were strictly limited to single-digit figures and others that weren't limited at all by volume.

It's your job to try these different avenues, understand that you probably won't get it right the first time, and remember that much of marketing and getting new things in front of your customers is going to involve a little bit of trial and error. The sooner you start testing these, then the quicker you'll get to the pot of gold.

If you happen to have a team of staff, then I'd also recommend that you involve them in this process as much as you can.

Not only did many of our best ideas come from our girls but also they felt involved and a part of the team by having their voices and ideas heard. They are also far more likely to get onboard and upsell and cross-sell experiences that they've had a hand in creating! Get them involved, make it fun and enjoy the benefits that come from consulting with a group of different people, each with different experiences to yours.

If you'd like Hollie's personal help with this, then that's available too. Every month, our Salonology Gold Club members get access to The Oracle, which is a monthly training session based around this very idea in which Hollie comes up with ideas, inspiration, seasonal themes and so much more that you can then interpret for your business.

It's the closest we've ever offered to done-for-you marketing.

Find out more at **www.salonologygoldclub.com**

✓ **SOMETHING TO MODEL** – Get your audience excited about what you're doing every month and give them an incredible reason to return more regularly. People will, if you make it interesting and appealing enough for them.

✘ **SOMETHING TO AVOID** – Hugely discounted services. This is not about offering £1 treatments or services in the hope that people will go on to buy something more expensive. That attracts all the wrong people.

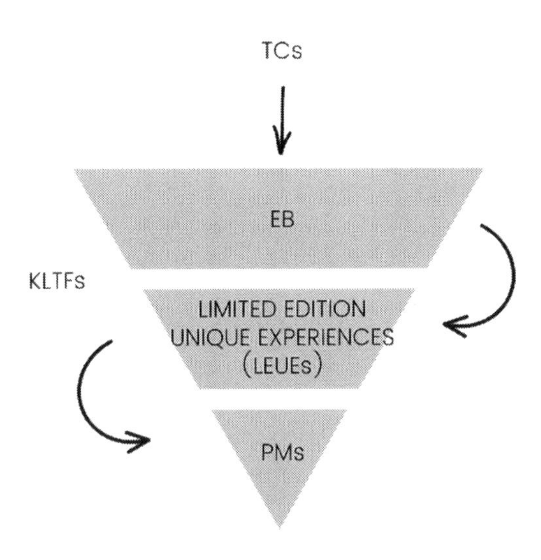

The first piece of your System is now in place

CHAPTER 6

EMAIL: AN UNEXPECTED SECRET SAUCE

Most businesses already have enough clients, despite many believing that's not the case.

It's been said before that you only need around 200 clients to have an incredible business – if those 200 clients spend enough with you and also buy regularly.

This was certainly the case for us. We knew that we had a great relationship with our clients – and that they loved to visit us; however, we needed them to spend more money and spend it more frequently. This was one of the driving forces behind our LEUE strategy.

The problem is that so many clients didn't get the memo; they don't realise that they need to keep returning time and time again at a rate that suits us, rather than them.

As business owners, it's our job to remind our clients to do business with us; it's not their job to remember. In the 21st century, attention spans are at an all-time low. It has been estimated that the average North American (sadly, I can't find a UK equivalent statistic so you'll have to run with that one) sees between 5,000 and 10,000 advertisements every day.[4]

Yes, every day!

That includes website banner ads, social media ads, radio and television commercials, newspaper and magazine advertisements, billboards and so much more.

That's a lot. Is it any wonder that so many people forget about the business owner who is only putting something in front of their clients once per week?

We knew that regular contact with clients was paramount to us encouraging them to come and visit us more often. The good news was that we now had something wonderful to tell them about. It'll be the same for you too when you put into place the strategy discussed in the previous chapter.

I recently heard the saying "The more you connect, the more you collect" – and I totally agree with that.

Many people get a proverbial bee in their bonnet regarding the idea that people will be turned off if we're in touch too often. I can understand why some may think that way, but I'd encourage you to test that for yourself to see if it's really true.

To begin with, people don't see everything you put out. Sure, you might do, but they don't. It might feel a lot for you if you're reaching out all of the time, but I promise you that people are busy. I mean they are *really* busy, and if you're only in irregular communication with your clients, then they are going to forget about you very quickly indeed.

Now it's true to say that people will soon turn off if you're boring, talk constantly about the same thing or if you're aggressively selling all the time, so it's really important to find different angles and stories to wrap around your content.

People do need to hear the message more than once – a lot more than once in the vast majority of cases; however, they don't need to hear it in exactly the same way each time. It's widely acknowledged within the marketing world that a client who doesn't know whom you are will take up to 20 'touches' (points of contact) before they are ready to do business with you.[ii,5] That means they need to see your name 20 times, including watching a couple of videos, reading some reviews, seeing some case studies or whatever it may be.

That's a lot.

Furthermore, most businesses give up way before that and aren't even giving clients a chance to take the next steps with them.

Not only that but it's also understood within marketing that people need to see your specific offer seven times before they are ready to dive in; this is sometimes called the 'Rule of Seven'. Again, that's a lot! Think about your own personal experiences: how many times have you seen an advertisement over and over again before you eventually dived in? I know that I've personally had things on my mind for months or more before, one day, I've gone for it, without consciously even knowing which touch tipped the balance for me. I'm sure it'll be the same for you.

Compare that with how many times you tell your clients about what you offer. A couple of social media posts that they may – but probably won't – see? An email here and there, or perhaps a mention in passing when they come into your salon? It's just not enough to help anyone but the really low-hanging fruit over the line.

Yes, merely increasing the volume with which you communicate with your current and future clients can sometimes be enough to increase your sales. Pretty simple, huh?

[ii] This actually goes back to the book *Successful Advertising* by Thomas Smith, which was written in 1885!.

There's a myriad of different ways that you can use to get your message in front of your clients (much more on that later in this book), but we've found great success using email. In fact, it's still my preferred method of communication.

Did you just roll your eyes right then? I hope not, and I trust we can still be friends, but I know that many feel email is dead. That it was the method of communication for a time that has passed.

Well, my friend, I'm here to tell you that email is very much still alive and kicking – when done correctly.

Back in the day, we used to send an email newsletter like everyone else did. It was just what you did back then. After all, all the big companies did that – and many still do – so it had to be right for us also.

Well, fast forward a few years, and it turned out it wasn't the best way for us to do it, and it's most likely not the best way for you to do it either. In fact, as you'll know if you read my first book, email newsletters are one of my pet hates.

I believe that, in order for us to want to make regular and repeat purchases from someone (which is what we want, remember), then we need to have some sort of relationship with them. I also believe that people buy people (also described as 'people buy from people'). Furthermore, they buy from people whom they know, like and trust.

Have you ever purchased something from someone you don't trust? I doubt it, and if you did, then I doubt you make regular purchases from them.

The problem is that it's difficult to build any sort of relationship with a newsletter. We just don't care. With this in mind, we started to change the way we sent emails.

We stripped out all of the images, the flashing text that was popular at the time, the bright colours, the fancy text and even our logo.

Shock horror! Were we mad? Well, maybe, but it all made sense in my head, so I was going to give it a try.

We started writing emails that looked like the ones you might send to your friends, rather than the sort normally associated with being sent by businesses.

People immediately recognise an email from a business and, straight away, their back is up. When we receive one of those, we always feel at the back of our minds that maybe there's some sort of ulterior motive going on here. I mean, why else would they be emailing me if they weren't trying to sell me something or get me to do something?

As a result, many of those emails are unopened or simply ignored. I knew we could do better, and it turns out that was accurate.

We wrote our emails specifically to look as though they were from one person to another person. To look like those emails we actually enjoy opening and reading: such as the one from our best friend seeing what we're up to this weekend, the one with the update on how our niece is doing at school or the invitation to the surprise birthday drinks. You know the ones.

We started to mimic these types of emails – except that the content was, of course, based around the salon.

You would not believe how much better a response you'll get to your emails when you adopt this approach, and I suggest you owe it to yourself and your business to at least give it a try.

Every single client of mine who has tried this has improved their results. They typically go from getting no engagement whatsoever to having people actually reply to their emails. Yes, people reply! Even though the email is actually being sent to hundreds or even thousands of recipients, people still take the time to type out a reply.

That's the start of a relationship right there. It's also a great way to build trust, get to know your clients better and to remain in their minds. It's also a brilliant way to sell a lot more of whatever your business does. Quite simply, it works.

If you currently send a newsletter-style email, then this is what I'd suggest, to see if it'll work for you too (which it will – I'm certain of that). You probably already have three or four things that you're going to share in your newsletter. Perhaps you've appointed a new staff member, perhaps there are roadworks outside your salon that you need to tell people about, or perhaps you have a new treatment you want to announce.

Rather than cram all of those into one difficult-to-consume (and easy-to-ignore) newsletter, break all of those up into separate weekly emails. For each email you send, make it about one thing. Have one topic and make it bite-sized. Remember, people are busy. Many won't have time to read thousands of words, so don't put that upon them. Sometimes, my emails are only a few lines long. Just like an email from a friend is sometimes only a few lines long.

Where possible, spin your news and turn it into a story. People love stories, and people love other people who can tell them. Now I know there's every chance that you don't consider yourself much of a storyteller. That's fine, because nobody does. The truth of the matter, however, is that you're perfectly able to tell a good-enough one. After all, you've been telling them all your life.

As humans, we are hardwired to engage with and respond to stories. From the dawn of time cavemen (and women) sat around fires telling stories. They drew them on the walls of caves. The Bible is made up of them. As children, we heard one nightly if we were good. Even now, the vast majority of us come home and are greeted with "How was your day?" – to which we normally respond with...

That's right – a story.

Stories are all around us. They are the backbone of human connection. They are happening everywhere, and as a business owner, we shouldn't be short on material.

One of the major mistakes so many make is thinking that people won't care about your stories. I promise you that many will. In fact, they'll love them. You'll be surprised at how many people are reading them – and they will even comment on them when they see you next (which, of course, will be more regularly than before!).

Storytelling is a learnable skill. As Brian Tracy says, "If you can drive a car, then you can learn the skill." Learning to drive is one of the toughest skills to learn as a total novice, and yet the vast majority of the population manage it (admittedly, some need more lessons than others, and some probably shouldn't have a licence at all, but that's a discussion for another day).

We are all novice storytellers to begin with. It's fine to start at the beginning. It's where every novice starts – and remember, all experts were once beginners.

The best thing to do is simply to start, and then practice. There's no need to overthink it. With time, you'll find your style, you'll get better at it, and you'll enjoy it more and more – especially when you see the bookings and sales coming through as a direct result.

It surprises many people when I tell them that email was our number one source of bookings for our salon. Not Instagram, not Facebook and not Google. Email. Good ol' free-to-use email. That's not to say we didn't do the other things (we did, as you'll find out later) but email beat them all hands down.

Now, you're not going to go from people not reading them (and buying nothing) to them devouring each email you send the moment they receive it (and buying everything). As humans, we don't typically operate like that. To begin with, people will quietly be watching on the sidelines. They won't be used to receiving this type of email. Not from you, and not from many businesses. Most businesses are still doing the newsletter-style ones – if anything at all.

This becomes an area where you can make some wonderful gains. You're going to stand out like a beacon in their inbox. If they choose to open and read only one of their emails from you, then you've got a chance. A much better chance than if you're sending an email with the subject line of "Newsletter for May". I mean, seriously! Only the most ardent of followers is going to open something like that. Most people don't care about your news. Bizarrely, however, they will care about your stories – especially when they can relate to them.

The formula I prescribe for emails is very simple. There's no need to complicate things when you don't need to.

First, consider the end goal. What's the action you want people to take at the end of the email? It might be making a booking online, it might be watching a video or it might be replying to signal interest in something. Whatever it is, consider that first. Most emails we sent would have an end goal of some sort.

Next, you want to work backwards and think of a way that you can tie that action in with a story. This is the part that many struggle with, but I promise you that the link can be fairly tenuous. If I want people to watch a short video about a new treatment, for example, then I could tell a story about a film I watched the night before and simply link the two with a transition phrase such as, "If you love video too, then have a quick look at this. It's only a couple of minutes long."

It doesn't matter that the video isn't about the film that you watched. The story you told will have lowered the guard of the reader and brought them closer to you. Some will then click on it, and some won't – and that's all good.

You might also want to mix this up a little, and you probably won't want to tell a story with each and every email. Sometimes, you might want to share a useful tip or help out in some other way.

We were almost exclusively promoting our LEUEs in our emails. Not blatantly – they were mostly hidden away after the story or in the PS at the bottom. We would sometimes email five to ten times per month to promote it in one way or another. Now, I know that some people will have just dropped the book or fallen off their chair. You may have even audibly shrieked on the bus. (If you did, you should probably apologise to the sweet little lady sitting in front of you.)

Won't you annoy people? I wouldn't want that many emails! What if people unsubscribe from my email list? *Argh!* The horror!

We did a fair amount of testing around email frequency, and this is what we found: the more emails we sent, the more sales and bookings we made.

Originally, we were pretty slapdash at sending our emails and would send them only once per month at best. That was the norm back in the day.

So we decided to see what would happen if we sent them more frequently. After all, much of marketing is seeing what works for you and your audience. We upped it to twice per month, and we found that more people opened them, read them and replied to them. Most importantly of all, they also made more bookings.

So we upped it again, to weekly. The same results occurred. We tried twice weekly, and again, this resulted in more bookings than before. We tried three times per week and found that we had a little resistance to that. We had only marginally more bookings and lots more unsubscribes.

Two emails per week was our sweet spot. Now, that's not to say that'll be your sweet spot – there's no one-size-fits-all approach – but you do need to push the boundaries and see what works for you. If you're paralysed with what to write and find yourself staring at a blank screen for hours, trying to grind out a few lines, then I'd suggest that it isn't the best use of your time and you may want to rein that in a little.

Conversely, if you find writing them easy and enjoyable, and you're getting great results, then why not consider sending even more? Funnily enough, if we still had the salon, then I'd probably experiment again with a much higher frequency. At the time of writing this, I send emails to large sections of our email list every day. Yup, every single day. Do some people unsubscribe? Sure they do, but that's okay because plenty of others buy.

There are some business owners who get very upset about people unsubscribing from their email list. They take it really personally, as if they've really offended someone or believe it means that client won't come in any more. For the most part, neither of those are likely to be true.

There are lots of reasons why people unsubscribe, but that's not enough in itself to stop emailing the others. The rewards of all the other additional bookings greatly outweigh the cost of some people opting out, in my opinion.

I also believe that, if someone really doesn't want to receive communications from me, they'll probably not go on to be one of my best customers. If my message is really missing the mark with them – or they just don't care – then that's fine, but were they ever going to purchase? It's best we send the communications to those who are excited to hear from us and ready to take us up on our offers. As many will do.

Now I'm fully aware that email isn't perceived as being all that sexy any more (if it ever was). Other technologies have come along, and you may prefer to do much of your communication via text message, WhatsApp or whatever the latest technological advancement is. I'm not against using any of those, and they all have their place. However, I am a firm believer that email still has a place in your overall strategy.

I've yet to find a better communication tool in which I can spend just a few minutes a day (or a week) to send one message to thousands of people at one time, which can lead to lots and lots of bookings. We've had more than 100 bookings from one single email in the past – but more on that in the next chapter (Chapter 7).

It's perfect for building relationships, building trust and making sales. Oh, and it's pretty much free too.

I don't say 'completely free', as I'd actually recommend using proper email software, most of which you have to pay a small monthly fee for. The reason I say this is because, due to General Data Protection Regulation (GDPR), you need to have an unsubscribe link in your emails so that people can opt out. If you're sending from Gmail, Hotmail or any free account, then you won't have that, and technically, you could be opening yourself up for some problems.

Cover your backside and grab an account with recognised software. You'll find they have lots of other cool features for the most part too, such as being able to add people's names into the text and split test different subject lines to see which works the best.

I personally use ConvertKit, but you might want to check out Mailchimp, MailerLite or ActiveCampaign, depending on your needs.

There's one final – and very important – reason why I love email so much:

You own the data.

Once someone has subscribed to receive your emails and given you authority to email them (again, this is much easier with a proper software provider), then you can contact them as you see fit.

It's not like social media, where at the drop of a hat, your posts won't be seen, the network will go down or your account is taken from you. All of which can happen, by the way.

If you're building your business entirely on social media, then you'll want to be careful. What happens if Mr Zuckerberg decides that, from now on, all pages have to pay to play? Or he moves the goalposts? Or he decides that you've broken a rule and removes your page? Heck, how about the idea that the entire website is taken offline?

They are all real issues we face, and I'd rather have more peace of mind than that. I know that if any of my accounts were taken down overnight, then I'd still have my list and I could still be in contact with all of my clients.

Most business owners already have the data for their clients; they just don't use it to the full effect.

For us, we knew we were on to something. What we needed to figure out next was how we were going to grow that list so that we could reach even more clients.

For my complete course on sending simple emails that sell – and my formula for content creation made easy – check out our Salonology Gold Club.

Find out more at **www.salonologygoldclub.com**

✓ **SOMETHING TO MODEL** – It's much easier to get your message heard when there's less noise. Go where the others aren't.

✗ **SOMETHING TO AVOID** – Not sending enough email, which is one area that so many salons can improve upon and enjoy the benefits immediately.

CHAPTER 7

RUNNING COMPETITIONS THAT ACTUALLY WORK

Capturing the email addresses of your clients – and having their explicit authorisation for you to email them – should be one of your primary tasks as a marketer. It will, as discussed, help you to build stronger relationships with your clients – which, in turn, will help you to make more sales.

The best possible way I've found to do this is to capture this information via your website.

It sounds easy enough, but there is one problem: clients have become wise as to why you want their email address. They know that there are plenty of unscrupulous marketers out there who will simply bombard them with unwanted spam. If you can believe that!

In order to collect someone's email address, we need to give them a good reason to go ahead and complete that data-capture form. We need to give them something that they value more than their email address. I like to call this an ethical bribe (EB).

I call it that because, in essence, what we're doing is swapping what we have (more on that in a moment) for what they have (their email address).

This is nothing new, and you'll see this on company websites all the time. You might have even signed up for a couple this very week.

Once upon a time, it was enough simply to ask people for their details in order to receive your newsletter, but that doesn't work too well now – not least because people don't really want your newsletter. We need to do better than that. We need a better lure.

Your EB should generate you leads, ideally be free (or very inexpensive) for you to deliver and have a high perceived value (so people actually register for it).

In the past, we've tested plenty of different EBs (which are also sometimes referred to in some circles as 'lead magnets'), from a free report to a video series to a money-off voucher.

Free reports can be a great way to collect information. Provided that the report contains something that is of value to your client or solves a specific problem that they have, then these can work. A simple, two-page PDF, for example, on 'Nine Ways To Make Your Skin Look Radiant in the Winter' might be enough to tip some people over the edge into giving you their email address.

They are pretty much free to do, require little to no technology (type them out in Word and simply save as a PDF) and can be created very quickly. You might even want to create several of these to appeal to different audiences.

Additionally, they also position you as an expert. Being viewed as a go-to expert in your field is a wonderful place to be and is highly recommended. Experts get more enquiries, have more people take their recommendations, get fewer complaints and – possibly the most attractive of all to you – can charge more.

A video series can have a similar effect. Again, it can place you as an expert or authority figure, and it is a great way to show your clients both your level of expertise and how you can help them with whatever they are struggling with. It also has the added benefit of them actually being able to see you on their screen.

Remember that people buy people. They'll be even more likely to buy from you when they can see you. We respond to faces and voices – especially those that we recognise. If you're doing a lot of online video, then this might be a smart strategy for you.

The difficulty here is getting people to consume the content. Sending people an hour's worth of video is more likely to switch them off than turn them on (when did you last have time for that?).

Whilst I see lots and lots of salon owners offer discount vouchers on their websites, this isn't a strategy I'd recommend. Just because others do it doesn't necessarily mean it's a great idea.

To begin with, it positions you right from the outset as someone who will give a discount if the right person asks in the right way. Compare how that sits to someone who positions themselves as an expert. When you start the relationship in this manner, you can expect those same clients to ask for discounts regularly. After all, you've trained them to believe that you offer them. Remember, we want to add value where we can and not discount.

(A quick side note about discounts: when you give someone a discount, then that money is coming directly from your pocket. Your costs remain the same, so it's pure profit that you're willingly handing over to anyone who asks. Taking £10 off here and 10% there soon adds up over the course of a year, and it could be taking thousands of pounds straight from your profits – profits that you could invest in new equipment, staff training, a holiday or anything else you care to spend it on.)

If you're giving discounts to your clients – especially without a good reason or just because you always have – then I'd encourage you to stop that behaviour as soon as possible. Like, today. Even for those clients whom you've served for years and even for your friends. Actually, especially for your friends. If they want to support your business – and I hope they do – then the least they can do is actually pay the going rate. I mean, seriously!

Here's a way to think about it that I hope will prevent you dishing out discounts hand over fist ever again. When someone asks for – or is offered – a discount of, say, £10, mentally picture yourself taking it out of your purse or wallet and giving them the cash from there.

Doesn't feel so good, does it? Yet this is exactly what you're doing. You almost certainly wouldn't stop Mrs Goggins in the street and hand over your hard-earned money, so don't do it in your salon. Remember, you need to make a profit or you've got an expensive hobby and not a business.

There are plenty of other options you might wish to consider too, and one size doesn't fit all. You might want to try a cheat sheet, top-tip list, planner, workbook, tutorial or any number of other things. As long as it is of value to whomever you're trying to attract, then it's worthy of a trial.

Whilst we had a reasonable amount of success with giving away short-and-sharp reports that we felt our clients would find useful, it wasn't quite cutting the proverbial mustard for us. In true marketeer fashion, we decided to try something new again.

This time, we nailed it. Over the course of the next few years, we ran exactly the same EB on our website month in and month out. In fact, it was so successful that, at one point, we'd managed to collect over 9,000 email addresses. Even after that list was ravaged by GDPR, we still retained well over 6,000. Again, that's not bad at all. In fact, it's much better than not bad. The ability to be able to put our message in front of so many people at will, and for very little cost, should not be underestimated. Remember, these were people from whom we were garnering their trust by way of our personal and chatty emails.

So, what did we do? We ran a competition every month to win a spa day for two people.

Now, on the face of it, that might seem like a fairly generous prize. It was; the same prize would cost a few hundred pounds if someone were to purchase it. However, that's an important factor, as if the prize were of little or no value, then not as many people would enter the competition. We had a large spa, with lots of diary columns to fill, so we were looking to attract as many people as possible.

You may have tried running competitions for your business before – after all, they are hardly anything new or revolutionary. We all see them on social media all day long: tag this, share that and comment here.

This was different, however. The goal for us was to collect email addresses. Lots of them. We weren't after meaningless social media engagement from people who would never become a client, and we weren't about to run competitions that broke the Facebook rules either (and I don't recommend you do that either).

We felt that, if we could collect email addresses and nurture all of those who didn't win, enough of them would become clients to make the whole thing profitable. That turned out to be true. Of course, not all of them did, but that was fine. Enough did. More than enough.

Sometimes, it might take people a year or more to finally set foot into our business. Sometimes, people would just unsubscribe right away. Sometimes, we'd end up with a client for life.

Sometimes, business is a numbers game, and you need to test things, speculate, and accept that some things will work and others won't.

Here's exactly how we did it, so that you can adapt it for your own business if you wish.

First, choose a prize. We did the same prize every month, simply because it required less administration for us. If you're committed to doing a monthly LEUE, then you could just as easily choose that as your prize. Just make sure you're running your numbers and you know that what you're giving away isn't worth more than the business you're bringing in as a result.

For us, a spa day for two was perfect. It was enough of a pull to make people sign up, and it also meant that the winner was able to bring a friend along. That gave us a chance to convert another person into a loyal customer. Potentially, this was someone we didn't yet have access to or someone who'd never heard of us at that stage. Coming with a friend also meant that they were likely to enjoy the experience more, as well as being more likely to take photos of each other having a great time – photos that they'd frequently share on social media whilst tagging us, which was again putting our name in front of even more of their friends.

Choosing a spa day also meant that we didn't get as many people entering who could never realistically become a client. We didn't want loads of people from Glasgow entering when we were based in Bournemouth, and this helped to control that. Why would someone even enter the competition if they weren't prepared to travel however far it was to visit us?

This is also why I'd recommend against giving a prize that can be posted. If you offer skincare or a hairdryer, for example, then you could feasibly have people enter from all over the world, and all you're going to end up with is a list of people who will never become clients (and, potentially, a large postage bill). That's literally the opposite of what we're trying to achieve here.

Next up, we had to consider how we would select a winner. To again ease the administrative burden, we simply made people enter once, and then they'd be entered every single month for as long as they remained on our email database. Forcing people to enter month after month was pointless and unnecessary.

We held our prize draw on the first day of each and every single month, and we simply pulled a name out of a hat from all the entrants. An actual hat too, although there are now plenty of computer programs that will gladly pick you a randomised winner if you'd prefer something a little more technologically advanced.

I really wouldn't overthink this bit too much. Many people whom I've shared this with worry that people will ask for proof of who won or question the validity of any winners. Not once did that happen to us in years of doing this. Seriously, people just don't care as much as you might suspect.

How we announced the winner was one of the major keys to the success of this. Now, you could do a Facebook Live or something similar and pick a winner that way. In my experience, most people who enter aren't always prepared to sit and watch a video. There is also every chance that they will never see the video as Facebook (or any other social media platform) won't, of course, show the video to everyone. If 5% of your followers see it, then you're doing really well.[iii] Cue the eye rolls.

[iii] This figure comes from my own experience and from speaking with hundreds of salon owners' experiences and comparing them with my own.

Instead, we sent out an email on the first of each month to announce it there. Remember, we had the email addresses of everyone who had entered. Furthermore, upon them entering, we'd send them a little automated message saying they were in the hat, letting them know that we picked our winners on the first of every month and telling them to look out for that email each time. We also included it in the competition terms and conditions – something you'll want to add to your website somewhere. Most likely, nobody will ever read them, but they're there to protect all parties, and it helps to ensure that what you're doing is all above board. You can pretty much put whatever terms and conditions you want; we simply found an online template and tweaked it to suit us.

Now, if you'd entered a competition – which presumably you wanted to win – would you open an email from the organisers with the subject line of "The winner is..."?

Of course you would! So did our audience. Lots of them.

It wasn't uncommon for us to get open rates of 40–50% on that email each month. To put that into perspective, it's widely accepted in marketing circles (and backed up by my own experience) that if you get 20% of people opening your emails then you're doing pretty well. Furthermore, that percentage gets lower and lower the more subscribers you have. Therefore, for us to get up to 50% to open that email – potentially up to 4,500 real people who lived somewhere nearby – well, this was huge for us.

Here's the secret sauce that made it so effective for us. The bit that really used to get us excited. The real reason why we chose not to announce the winner by any means other than a good old-fashioned email.

As you'll remember, we used to run our LEUE every month. We used to also first announce that via email.

Can you see where this is going? I'm hoping a giant light bulb has just lit up above your head.

On the first of each month, we'd fire out an email. The subject line would suggest that the chosen winner was named inside, which they were. However, we'd have that right at the bottom. Before the reader could get to that big reveal, they'd first have to read all about that month's LEUE. Potentially, thousands of pairs of eyeballs were reading this every month.

Now, of course, one person would get to the bottom to discover they'd won, which was wonderful. The rest? Well, they hadn't, but perhaps they might be interested in this strictly limited off-menu experience that we were also offering. Naturally, they'd have to speak up quickly if they were interested, as not only was it only available to book that month but we also only had a limited number of spaces available.

We included a link to our booking software in the email, and if they wanted to click on that and pay a 50% booking fee, then their space would be reserved.

Every month they booked in droves. One month, over 100 people booked just from that first email. That was worth over £5,000 in bookings to us in one morning. Not bad, eh?

The whole system was set up to get that LEUE in front of them. Doing it this way, they were far more likely to open it – and do so excitedly too. From that email, they had three outcomes: they won; they didn't win, but they might want to book this cool LEUE; or they didn't win and weren't interested, but would be in with another chance the following month.

It really was a win-win situation.

We had ourselves a marketing system. We knew that if we poured enough leads into the top of it, then we could use email to make friends with these people using our chatty and informative style, and some of those people would become clients. Due to our LEUEs, we also knew that many of those clients would actually become amazing regular guests – to the extent that some used to book in blindly every month before they even knew what the experience was. Pretty cool, especially when you consider the entire system cost us hardly anything to run.

What we had to figure out next was how we could get even more people into our System...

✓ SOMETHING TO MODEL – Sending email. Sure, it might not be the sexiest or the most popular form of marketing, but it works and it'll help to make you a lot more money. Something that works trumps something that is fashionable, all day long.

✗ SOMETHING TO AVOID – Monthly newsletters. They are boring, they excite nobody, and with just a couple of subtle tweaks, you can do so much better and make twice the impact.

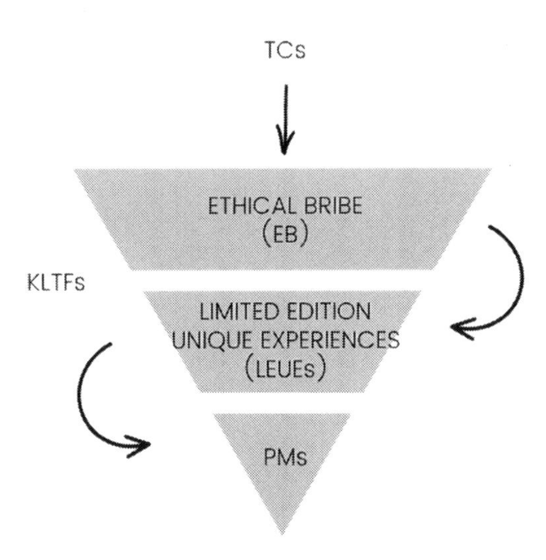

Your System is now coming together

CHAPTER 8

DOMINATING FACEBOOK

Once we'd realised that we were on to something with our strategy for filling our salon, we had to turn our attention to getting more exposure.

Just like today, the marketplace was a crowded one, with tens of salons in our home town of Bournemouth and literally hundreds of hotels – many with spas, salons and beauty rooms attached.

Social media was not quite the behemoth that it is today; however, Facebook was certainly already popular and was being used by many of our target dream clients. It was also very easy at this time to get right in front of exactly whom we wanted – whether they were already an existing client or not.

I mentioned earlier (see Chapter 6) that email was our number one way to turn strangers into clients, but running it a close second at that time was Facebook.

As social media is a landscape that changes so very quickly, I'll try to keep more to the strategies that we used rather than the specific tactics. The tactics will come and go depending on the platform algorithm; however, the strategies that underpinned what we did are likely to be more useful for you to model.

One of the keys to success on any social media platform is engagement. It's the fuel that fires the algorithm and is the one thing more than any other that will ensure your name stays in front of your clients.

That in itself is a comment worth exploring further. As mentioned earlier in the book (see Chapter 6), it can take your client seeing your presence up to 20 times before they are ready to move forwards with you.[6] Furthermore, in our industry, the buying cycle is also important. There are only certain times that your clients will ever be ready and willing to invest their time and money with you. It doesn't matter how good your marketing is – if someone has had a manicure yesterday, then they aren't going to have another one today. This is why it's so important to stay at the front of your clients' minds: when your client is ready, you're the first name they think of.

Let's first take a look at the basics of how the algorithms work on social media. Whilst the specifics and inner workings of them not only change but are also closely guarded, here's a breakdown of the basics so that you can start to use them to your advantage.

I like to think of the algorithm as a little robot. We'll call him (or her or them – I'm all up for equal robot opportunities) Mickey, after Metal Mickey (ask your parents). This little robot determines who is shown what posts and when. There are certain things you can do that will please Mickey – and certain other things that will make him upset.

First, we need to understand that Mickey works for Mark Zuckerberg and not for us. The goal for Facebook – as it is for any business, including yours – is to make a profit. In the case of Facebook, it makes its money by selling advertising space on the network. In order to do this, it needs to keep its users on the site for as long as possible. The more time people spend on the platform, then the more advertising space is available, the more adverts will be clicked on, and the more money Mr Zuckerberg and his shareholding cronies make.

Mickey is there to help ensure that people remain on the platform and don't get distracted by other apps, websites, videos of cats playing the piano or anything else on the internet.

Mickey is smart. Mickey is able to learn what people like and what they don't, based on their user behaviour. This includes understanding what they click on, what they engage with and what types of videos they consume. All of this information is collated cleverly, so that in the future, Mickey will show you more of what he perceives you to like and less of what he perceives you don't. For the most part, we'd have to say Mickey does a pretty good job of this, which means people spend longer and longer on the platform.

One of the main signalling factors to Mickey is the content we engage with and how we engage. For example, have you ever noticed that if you click 'like' on a post, you then start seeing more posts from that creator? Often, this happens whether or not you even follow them. This is because Mickey is making the assumption that, if you like the first thing, you'll probably like the second one also. It's the same for other similar content, even from completely different creators.

So, as a business owner, one of the main things we can do to ensure that our content is seen regularly by the right people is to try as best as we can to get people to engage with it. Engagement might mean hitting the like button, leaving a comment or simply watching more than a few seconds of a video.

It gets better too, as this compounds. When lots of people engage with a post, this is telling Mickey that this is good content, and therefore Mickey will then show the post to even more people. Hurrah for Mickey!

The opposite, however, is also true. If hardly anyone engages with the content, then this is a signal that others are unlikely to enjoy it either, and therefore the post will hardly be shown to anyone.

This is why the first 20 to 30 minutes after posting are the most crucial. If you get lots of early engagement, then you'll have a winning post on your hands, but if there is nothing at all on your post in those early stages, then you can expect it to die a quick (and painful) death.

So, we now understand that engagement is king (or queen, if you prefer) and is also the lifeblood for your page staying active. When you conquer this, then your page will not only grow but also will flourish. Similarly, this is the way that some pages die out. The engagement on the posts simply gets lower and lower until the posts are seen by nobody, and the page effectively fizzles out like a damp sparkler on Guy Fawkes' Night. It's a sad way to bow out, for sure.

Whilst there were some very specific types of post we used to share all of the time, I want to steer away from this intricate detail, as typically, these types of tactics will only work on social media for a short period of time. You need to keep ahead of the game. One way to do this is to keep an eye on what other accounts are doing. Not salons necessarily, but the people who are using social media as their main source of income.

What types of posts do you see these larger accounts making? What is getting lots of attention and engagement? What isn't? You can learn a lot from both the successes and failures of others. That said, nothing beats your own testing, and you'll want to test a lot of things. Some will work great, and some won't. That's simply how it is.

One great way to elicit engagement is by asking more questions. As human beings, we're hardwired to want to respond to questions – especially when we know the answer. We just can't help ourselves. We're like seven-year-old Ryan sitting up front in class, trying to stretch his hand even closer to the ceiling to get the attention of the teacher. Almost jumping out of our seats – with sound effects to match.

Your audience will be like that too when you pose the right questions to them. One of the questions I get asked a lot is whether these questions themselves need to be salon related in some way or another. Personally, I'd advise that you mix it up a little.

Here's the thing: if you ask questions about the salon, people's skincare routines, what their concerns are, new treatments they'd like to see and that kind of thing, then yes, the information you receive back will be more helpful. However, that's not the reason we're asking the questions. The reason is because we want engagement on the page to appease Mickey the robot.

When you ask questions that are difficult to answer, require more than a moment's thought, or are sensitive or personal in nature, then you can expect the number of people prepared to answer to go through the floor – especially on a Facebook page, as people understand that it is a public forum.

Who wants the rest of the world to know they secretly suffer from adult acne, for example? Not many people at all, unsurprisingly.

However, they will be more than happy to tell you where they are going on holiday, what they had for breakfast or what they will be eating for Christmas lunch.

I know this may seem somewhat futile to some. After all, business is serious business, right? Well, it is for some. I believe that if you have a little fun with it, then it actually becomes a lot more enjoyable – both for you and your clients. I am a firm believer that the voice of your business shouldn't only talk about business. After all, you're so much more than that. A salon is often a hub of the community; it's somewhere that people go to unwind, relax and let off steam. It doesn't need to be entirely serious all of the time, unless you want it to be.

Here's the other thing with those questions: they'll drive the engagement – and remember, that's what we want. In fact, it's what we need. It's essential. Without it, your page will go backwards in terms of growth, and you'll be resorting to paying for all of your posts to be seen. That's not only expensive but also unnecessary. It's often what's already happened to all those folks that you see shouting, "*Facebook is dead!*" It's not. They just don't understand the rules of Mickey's game.

This playful approach should ideally sit alongside other things you're posting too. If you're always posting about the business, then you're also going to run out of material pretty quickly, as well as turning your clients off.

Even the most ardent of your business's fans want you to post about something other than your work. In fact, they crave it the most. They want to see the inner workings. What's behind the scenes. The people involved. Don't leave all of that out; it's so important.

It's these things that help to ensure that more people know, like and trust you; this is why I call things such as this 'know, like and trust factors' (KLTFs). These KLTFs are the key to people coming back more and more often. Everything is interlinked.

So many salon owners are scared to pull back the curtain; however, it's one of the simplest and most impactful things you can do for your business. People are nosey. Social media is entirely based on this principle. People watching what other people are doing – and often lurking in the shadows, hiding, whilst they do it! How many people immediately look up ex-partners, for example, on social media to see what they are up to? Spoiler alert: lots of people do!

Given that we understand people are nosey, but also that people buy people, it's my view that we should pander to this somewhat and give 'em what they want.

This is precisely why I'm advising you to step out from behind the camera a little and put yourself – and your team – in front of it. Talk about your team, discuss what you do in your downtime and inject a little personality into your social media. I promise you that it goes a very long way on so many levels.

When it comes to frequency of posting, there is no magic formula per se, and you'll want to test it for your own audience. What I've found over the years is that three posts per day seems to be the sweet spot for us. That might not be the same for you, and it'll not only change from platform to platform but also it'll probably have changed since the time of writing.

However many times per day you decide to post, then my advice is twofold. First, once you've found what works for you, stick to it. Being consistent is really important. In fact, it's important for success in any field, and it certainly applies here too. Being consistent with your posting not only keeps your audience engaged but also keeps your name in front of them – as well as keeping Mickey happy too.

Second, schedule as much in advance as you can. There's simply no need to be uploading posts on the fly every day. When you sit down and schedule them out in advance, you'll have a much higher quality of post – meaning you'll get more engagement and appreciation from your audience. You'll also be able to be way more strategic as you'll actually be thinking about what you're trying to achieve rather than just throwing something up there in between clients because that's better than nothing.

Who'd have thought that a little prior planning would be so effective, eh?

As part of our Salonology Gold Club, I've created a complete training video on this; it gives my method for creating three posts per day and getting them all scheduled in less than 60 minutes per week.

One part of that methodology I want to share with you here is my post-subject framework. You can use this as the starting point for what to post. Whilst I wrote it with Facebook in mind, much of it is translatable to other social media networks too.

I call it my **APOSTLES** method, which is, of course, a clever mnemonic designed to help you remember it. You'll remember that I recommend mixing up what you post and not making it all about your business. That is true here also.

The A stands for 'ask'. As you've learned, we're hardwired to answer questions, and this is a wonderful way to elicit engagement, which is something essential for the well-being and growth of your page. It's also something that you can have a little fun with.

Here's a couple of ninja tips for you when it comes to Mickey and the topic of questions. First, ask open-ended questions where possible. Questions that receive actual answers – rather than simply 'yes' or 'no' answers, or even emojis – will be favoured by the algorithm. This is even more true if you can encourage people to respond with full sentences or paragraphs. The more they respond, then the more of an interest signal this is to Mickey, and the happier he'll be.

The second ninja tip here is deliciously simple but really effective. It should go without saying that you'll want to reply to everyone who leaves comments on your posts. Unless they are trolling you, then it's just good manners.

When questions and answers are involved, however, there's an opportunity for you to take it to the next level. When someone answers your question, follow it up with another one. Normally, they'll answer that one too, and this is a huge flag to Mickey that this post is of interest. The back and forth is one thing that can send the reach of your posts through the roof.

Here's what that might look like:

> *Question posed by the page: "Where are you going on holiday this year?"*
>
> *Member of audience: "I'm going to Las Vegas."*
>
> *Page in response: "We love Las Vegas; which hotel are you staying at?"*
>
> *Member of audience: "We're staying in the Golden Nugget; it's our first time in that hotel!"*
>
> *Page in response: "That's a great hotel in a fab location. Have you been to Vegas before, then?"*

And so on and so forth.

This might seem pointless to you, but it's important on two levels. First, we're keeping Mickey happy, but almost more importantly, we're also creating deeper bonds with our clients.

When you next see that client, perhaps you and the team will remember they were going to Las Vegas. Perhaps you'll chat about it when they're in for their pre-holiday manicure. Maybe they'll even send you a postcard, if people still do that!

As Hollie always says, "Bonds build businesses." When you can get past the surface layers and find real common ground with your clients, then you can expect them to visit you with increased regularity, spend more money with you and refer you to their friends like crazy. This is just one way that you can help to future-proof your business.

P stands for 'personal'. As already touched upon, I thoroughly recommend pulling back the curtain a little and getting in front of your audience. This is a huge KLTF.

So many business owners hide behind their logo and don't want to put themselves out front. I really believe that this is a mistake. People buy people and not brands. It's very difficult for us to have any real connection with a logo, however pretty or pink or expensively designed it might be. It's very easy, on the other hand, for us to have a real connection with a person.

As humans, we actually crave those connections, and even more so since everything that's happened post-2020 (mostly due to the Covid pandemic). Give people a chance to connect with you, and they'll automatically be more likely to then connect with your business too.

(As a side note, this is true whether you have a team or not and whether you deliver the treatments or not. None of that matters. What matters is that you stand a better chance of making a connection with someone – and a better chance of them ultimately becoming a great client – when you actually show your face and your personality, rather than relying on your logo.)

Some business owners really struggle with this. Some also want to keep their business and personal lives separate. I do get this – but they'll see you when they set foot in your salon, right? Why not just put it out there from the start?

It is possible to hide away, of course, if you really wanted to. However, I would argue that your business will be more successful if you step out from behind that curtain a little more. You'll probably have more fun too.

As a local business owner, you'll actually be a little bit of a minor celebrity in your locale. I know that may sound weird if you've never thought about that before. But look at it this way: if you bumped into one of your clients anywhere other than your salon, then you'd say hello to them, right? That means they've recognised you – and that makes you a celebrity of sorts. Why not embrace that?

I'm not saying that you need to become a household name or a social media influencer, by the way. But I am saying that, if you're known in your area as the number one go-to person for XYZ, then your business will probably really benefit from that. Much more so than the faceless salon that isn't known for anything at all.

Within this category of posts, you can go as deep as you wish. If you're going to share it, then what you get up to outside of the salon will be of interest to your clients. As would photos of your dog, if you have one, and even your children.

I understand that some people are comfortable with this and some aren't, and that's fine. I'm not going to tell you to do something you really don't want to do, so find something that fits within your own comfort level.

I will say this, however: a photo of your child on their first day of school – or even a photo of the picture they drew on the first day of school – will garner more likes and more attention than any other you'll ever post, before or after. Fact.

I remember I was once speaking at an event and a member of the audience asked, "When I put up my 'before and after' pictures of my work, I hardly get any likes, yet when I put one up of my dog, I get lots. Why is this?"

Well, the answer is simple. Are you ready for this? People prefer dogs!

I mean, who wouldn't rather look at a photo of a cute little dog versus a couple of photos of someone's eyelashes (or whatever it may be)?

People are literally voting for what they want to see pictures of by tapping the like button. So you can tell what people want to see more of and less of. If I put up a picture and it received way more engagement than usual, then I'd definitely see how I could replicate that again. Use the information at your fingertips to be better at giving your clients (and Mickey too) what they want.

Now, to be clear, I'm not suggesting that you only post images of your dog and only ask questions about where people are going on holiday. I'm coming to the rest of the ideas. But I am suggesting that you mix it up a little. Most salon pages I see are literally hundreds and hundreds of client photos and very little else. Quite frankly, that's boring, and this is reflected in the growth the page is achieving and the reach those posts are generating.

O stands for 'ouch!' Ouch posts are where you're explicitly referencing pain points that your clients are experiencing. More specifically, these are pain points that you know you can help them with.

Let's say, for example, that your business offers cryolipolysis to your clients; aka fat freezing. As a business owner, you need to know all of the pain points that your treatment helps to solve. Why? Because this is the most powerful way you'll be able to garner your clients' interest and potentially sell them the treatment.

This is a huge part of what marketing is all about. You are letting your clients know that you understand they have a problem. You understand how they are feeling. And, by Jove, you're letting them know that you have a solution to that problem too.

Communicating with your clients in this way is going to be way more persuasive than simply throwing up a post with words to the effect of "fat freezing for £99" (something I sadly see far too much of).

Therefore, it's on us to understand deeply (or at least acknowledge) all of the different pain points that our clients could be experiencing.

Let's stick with the fat freezing example for the moment. People interested in fat freezing might be new mums who are struggling to shift the excess baby weight. Perhaps the real pain point for them, however, is the remarks that one of the other mums at the school gates has made.

That mum isn't going to respond to "fat freezing for £99", but she might read more about your "solution to make other mums at the school gates wonder how you've got so toned". See how this works?

You want to go a little deeper than the surface level and try to reveal what the real problems are, and to talk to your clients more in this language. When your clients see you as providing a solution to their problems, then you can expect to see them in your salon more.

As a business owner, you need to think long and hard about all the different pain points and problems solved by each and every treatment, product and service that your business offers. Start talking in these terms and watch how much more persuasive you become.

Remember the old adage: nobody wants a hammer; they want a nail in their wall.

It's the same for you: nobody wants fat freezing; they want to feel desired by their partner again like they were on their honeymoon, they want to be the mum who looks the best in shorts on sports day, or they want to have their girlfriends asking what their secret is at the next group brunch. More on this later (in Chapter 11).

(As a side note, I fully understand that may sound a little archaic, but they could be genuine pain points for your clients. You can use whatever examples you see fit for your clients, but I just want to stress the importance of going deeper here.)

S stands for 'specialist', and these types of posts are positioning you as the go-to expert in your field.

At this point, I'm going to assume that you are indeed an expert in what you do. If you don't consider yourself to be one, then you've got something to aim for. Many are already, but they just don't know it.

Many have years and years of experience (perhaps decades, even), have been on tens of advanced training courses, have a wall of certificates and have helped hundreds – or even thousands – of clients over the years.

Of course, I'm not talking about someone else bestowing the 'expert' label upon you; that particular crown needs to be self-claimed. If you begin to call yourself an expert, then others soon will too. Now, you can't really be an expert in lots of different fields, so pick the one that works for you. Perhaps you're a skincare expert. Perhaps you're a lash expert. Perhaps you're an intimate-waxing expert.

If you really want to stand out from the crowd and attract more clients with less resistance, then positioning yourself as the go-to expert is a really smart move (with the caveat being that you really are excellent at what you do, of course).

People want to work with experts, now more than ever. They don't want generalists. It's all a part of the modern celebrity culture, and the smart salon owner not only recognises this but also uses it to their advantage. As the local expert, specialist or even – dare I say – celebrity, you can expect a longer queue at your salon door than if all other things were equal and you didn't use that title. Seriously, that's the power of it.

Clients will climb over one another to get a piece of an expert. They'll boast to their friends, leave glowing reviews, take product recommendations and gladly pay whatever fee is commanded – such is the power of the expert status. Just look at how popular celebrity restaurants are (and how much they charge).

There's more good news too. Experts are not only sought out by clients but they also get far more opportunities than others. They're approached for their views by media outlets. Other business opportunities land in their lap. People want to work with them. They create a real buzz around themselves, and others are drawn to this.

This all begins with you. You need to claim this moniker for yourself. You should also be positioning yourself as the expert as much as you can in your social media posts.

This not only includes photos of the work you've carried out but also includes things such as sharing links to posts you've written, be those on your own website or someone else's. If you've been featured in a local magazine or newspaper, then this is great positioning (and if you haven't, then just reach out to them – it's really not as difficult as most people think). If you've entered awards for your business, then photos of you at the awards' nights – even if you don't win – also make great content for positioning you as the expert.

I know that some people really struggle with this idea of blowing their own trumpet. I'm not sure if it's an industry thing, a British thing or what. What I do know is that there's very little point having any sort of trumpet – be it a metaphorical one or a real one – if you're not going to blow it. You're awesome, and you're great at what you do. You change lives. Don't be afraid to give that trumpet a little toot every now and then.

T stands for 'testimonials'. Everyone understands the power and necessity of testimonials, reviews and case studies, and I am hereby encouraging you to share them whenever and wherever you can.

It's believed that a whopping 79% of shoppers will look for reviews before they make a purchase,[7] so don't be fooled into thinking some of those aren't your clients. Lots of them are no doubt, and especially the first-timers. Make sure that if people are looking – even with just one eye on your socials – then they are seeing the right things to take them over the line and assist their decision-making around booking that first appointment.

Every time someone says something nice about you online, you can screengrab that, crop it and use it as a social media post. If you're doing things right, you could potentially have many of these every day and build up a huge library of positive comments surrounding each of your treatments (and, ideally, the pain points they solve, as mentioned earlier). Perhaps they've been left as a review on Google or perhaps it's just a comment tagging you on your feed. It doesn't really matter either way, but get into the habit of screenshotting them and saving them somewhere for later use (assuming they weren't sent as a private message, of course). Future customers need to see these, and you can't have too many.

Testimonials and reviews are great – in fact, reviews are the lifeblood of your organic Google presence in many ways – but transformative case studies from clients will be some of the most powerful posts in your arsenal.

Case studies are more than just testimonials or reviews, as they have an added layer of emotion. We all make buying decisions emotionally – even if you don't think you do. As humans, we purchase emotionally and then justify rationally. That is, we come up with a list of logical reasons why we should indeed go ahead and make that purchase. It's the same for your clients, and this is why I spoke about tapping into their pain points earlier in this chapter. It's the same thing: tapping into the emotions.

When you have a client whom you believe would make a great case study for you and your business, simply ask them if they'd be happy to share their experiences with others. A few well-worded questions will be all you'll need, and most people will be happy to help.

To deliver the most punching power, your case study needs to follow your client on their journey. Like any good story, this will involve the main character (your client) going from a place of pain or discomfort to their new place of paradise. You want others to see this and believe that it's possible for them too.

You'll start with your client explaining where they were before you met. The pain they were feeling. The discomfort they were experiencing. Exactly how and why they were hurting so badly that they simply had to take action. This is really important, as it not only makes the great reveal of where they are now all that much more impressive but it will also resonate deeply with others who are currently experiencing this. Some of those people will eventually read this case study and want the same transformation for themselves. You're showing them the path.

After you've introduced your protagonist, then you'll describe your meeting with them as well as what you prescribed for them. You'll want to talk about what and why, as this will help to build up your position as the expert (and for the purpose of this story, you're the hero too!).

If the client has experienced any troubles or difficulties along the way, then include those too. They will help round the story out and not only make it more believable but actually make it more persuasive too. I mean, when does everything in life go exactly to plan?

After the client has spoken about their transformation (with photos, if possible, of course) then you'll want them to talk about the most important part: how they feel now.

This is the crux of the big transformation. It's not about how many inches their fat freeze took from them, it's all about how they felt before versus how they feel now. That's it.

Your transformational case studies will lay this journey out – and it's the foundation for all those potential clients in the future who feel like the client did at the start. Your case study shows them what's possible. It gives them hope. It helps them to understand that a brighter future is possible for them.

These types of posts are some of the most influential ones you'll upload. Ensure you have a variety of them, ideally referencing a variety of those pain points we spoke about before.

L stands for 'local interest', and it is one of the most underused types of post I see from this list.

If you're the owner of some sort of multinational conglomerate, then you can ignore this one; however, if you're the owner of a local business that serves your community, then this one's for you.

Funnily enough, this strategy came about completely by accident. When we still had our day spa and salon, there had been some roadworks announced by the local council. Roadworks that not only were going to be going on for what seemed like an unnecessarily long period of time but that were also going to be highly disruptive.

Like any good investigative journalists, those of our local rag, *The Bournemouth Echo*, were on the case and had published a story about it on their website. I've since learned that most local newspapers now operate in this way. They post frequently to their social media channels with each post containing a link to just one story on their website. (Naturally, they want you to click through to their website, which is where they now sell their advertising inches since the decline of the physical newspaper over the last decade or so.)

So, they'd written this story and shared the link on their Facebook page. In turn, we went and shared that link too, mostly as we thought it would be helpful to anyone coming for a treatment in the coming weeks (and potentially, months!).

Then everything went bonkers.

It turns out that a lot of people who followed our page – pretty much all local residents, of course – also had a view about these roadworks. I won't go as far as describing it as a public outcry or anything, but it was certainly something that a lot of people had an opinion about. An opinion they were keen to voice too.

Comments, shares, likes and new followers – the engagement went off the chart. I forget how many engagements that post had, but it was in the tens of thousands. All coming from a story that we didn't even write and wasn't about our business!

It was at this point that I realised perhaps we were on to something. After a little investigation, it turns out that I wasn't some sort of internet marketing supremo, but rather I had accidentally stumbled upon something known as 'news jacking' or 'news hacking'.

This is where you're putting a spin on events in the news to divert some of the attention to you. We found that this can work really well, especially at a local level. It's also perfect for people who never know what to post about or even those who don't enjoy writing, as someone else has already done the lion's share of the work – you're just adding your own spin or asking your audience for their take.

Here's how I now teach replicating this for your business. To begin with, go ahead and follow your local media outlets. Even smaller towns typically have a main newspaper (and possibly a free one too) and a couple of commercial radio stations, so this is something that everyone can replicate. If you have news where you are, you can do this. You have news, don't you?

Every few days – or whenever you're planning to post – scan their main Facebook business page. As noted before, most media outlets typically have one story per post. As you scroll down the page, you'll want to be looking at the engagement on the posts. Which ones have the most comments? Which ones have the most shares?

There are normally one or two standout posts that are getting lots of heat. These are the ones you want. If their audience is reacting to the story – for whatever reason – then yours probably will too.

Click on the post (don't hit the share button!) so that it takes you through to their website. You then want to copy and paste this URL into a brand new post. If you don't do this, then all the engagement (and the praise from Mickey) will go to the other page. Include the link along with whatever spin you want to add. For this reason, stories that are in some way linked to your business will typically perform the best. Our roadworks story worked well as people cared about this, but also because it impacted the roads immediately surrounding where we were based.

If you have strong business values or ethics on a certain topic (for example, you're a vegan salon or you only use 100% recycled materials), then stories reflecting these will not only perform well but also help to continue to carve you out as an expert or authority voice on these subjects. It's really simple but really effective – and you don't even need to do the heavy lifting on this one!

E stands for 'entertainment'. I've mentioned being boring earlier in this book. Elsewhere, I've described being boring as the number one marketing sin, and I stand by that today. Being boring makes life more difficult as a marketer, and entertainment is a good antidote to that.

You might have just broken out in a cold sweat. Perhaps you think that you're not entertaining or I'm suggesting you need to train to become a stand-up comedian to make this work for you. Thankfully, that's not required.

The type of entertaining posts I'm talking about crafting here are really just to break things up a little. To prevent everything being solely about business. Maybe it's a chance for you to inject a little personality into your brand, and this is certainly something to give people a reason to keep tuning in to your posts and content. I promise you that people will very quickly turn off from a feed of back-to-back 'before and after' shots, so you simply have to mix it up.

An entertaining post can be anything lighthearted or anything that makes someone break a smile. I, for one, certainly believe that the world could do with a little more of that kind of thing right now!

I've also taken the viewpoint that something that makes me laugh will probably make my target clients (TCs) laugh also; however, I do understand that might not be the case for you. Perhaps you have a business that is a little more serious than mine. Perhaps you deal in high-end aesthetics or offer semi-permanent make-up for cancer patients. Of course, you have to do what makes sense for your business – and the personality of your brand (which may be a little different to your own personality).

That said, I still believe there is room for a little fun every now and then. Business is best done with a smile on your face, and whilst you might not want to be sharing hilarious dog videos on your page on a daily basis, there are still some areas of common ground or observation that many of your clients will take humour from.

You have to try to make people look forward to seeing your posts, otherwise you will lose their interest very quickly. Making them smile is a wonderful way to do this, even if you're simply sharing the content of others.

The final letter of the mnemonic APOSTLES stands for 'stories'.

As discussed earlier, as human beings, we are hardwired to respond to stories. They are everywhere, they are relatable, and they are powerful when it comes to not only getting your point across but also building bonds with your audience.

As well as having a place in your emails, stories also have a place in your social media posting strategy. Heck, they can even be the same stories, if you like. There's no need to reinvent the wheel here, and repurposing content across multiple platforms is a smart strategy for the busy business owner.

On social media, you do have one extra string to your storytelling bow that you don't have on email, and that's the use of video. I mean, if a picture speaks a thousand words, then just how many would you attribute to a video? I guess we'd have to say a lot, right?

Plus, there's something else going on here that hasn't been touched upon just yet. There are two types of people who simply love video: both your audience and Mickey. More video is being consumed than ever before. Social media networks are being built purely on video. This drive is consumer led. People want to watch videos. They want to be entertained. They want to be distracted from everything else going on in their lives. They want to hear stories. They want to hear *your* stories.

As touched upon earlier, many people really get their proverbial knickers in a twist when it comes to storytelling. But what if the video only had to be short and simple? Not even a minute in length. I think that, with a little practice, anyone can do this. After all, we tell stories to one another literally all of the time:

"How was your day?"

"Well, this funny thing happened..."

Mickey also really loves those videos. If you get into the habit of sharing more video, then you can expect your engagement and your reach to go through the roof. Even just one per week would be great. Just to check in with your audience and let them know what you're up to. I promise you that they do care, even if you don't believe they do.

If you're sitting reading this and are thinking to yourself, *But, Ryan, I hate how I sound on video*, then you're not alone. Everyone I've met says the same thing, and there's a scientific reason behind that too. Everyone sounds different in their head to how they do on camera. It's all to do with the vibrations and the bone conduction within your head. Don't let that be an excuse to not get in front of a camera.

I promise you that, with a little practice, you will be great – and I also promise you that your clients will love it.

So there you have all the different categories of posts that I recommend and use myself. Mix them up a little, have a little fun with them and remember that you don't have to create all of the content you post. It's fine to post other people's stories and weblinks – just make sure that you credit them where appropriate. For photos and videos, you should really get copyright permission before posting them, though.

Keeping your feed fresh and your clients guessing about what you'll post next will not only give them plenty of reasons to keep coming back to your pages and feeds but it'll also make Mickey happy too – and as a business owner, you want him on your side. When the algorithm has your back, then it means more of your posts will be seen by the right people at the right time. That, in short, gives you more appointment-booking and money-making opportunities.

You might not like Facebook, and I get that. Maybe you prefer Instagram. Perhaps, since writing this, there's even there is a new kid on the block and everyone is downing their tools to rush over there. It matters little. Most of what I just laid out for you in terms of types of content to create will work on any social media platform. The principles remain the same, even if the logo on the app differs.

✓ **SOMETHING TO MODEL** – The key to social media is engagement. One of the very best ways to achieve this over the long term is to show and talk about more personal subjects. Your clients want to know the face behind the brand. It's a cornerstone of success for local businesses, and yet it's one that is so commonly overlooked.

✘ **SOMETHING TO AVOID** – Making your social accounts boring. There's nothing that will turn your clients off faster than seeing the same old things every time you post. And yes, that includes 'before and after' photos.

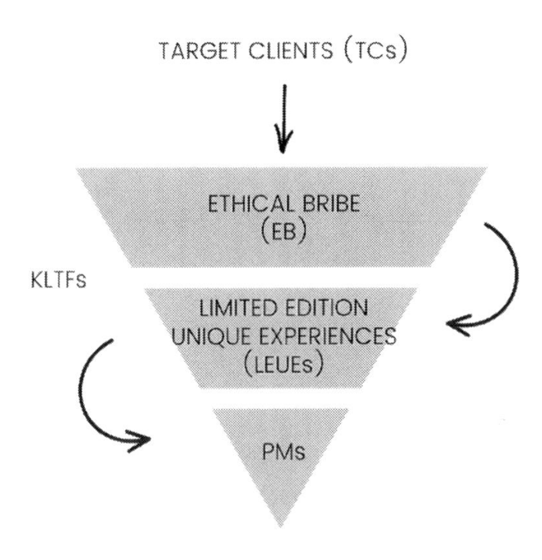

Piece by piece, your System is coming together

CHAPTER 9

RUNNING ADS

Sadly, social media has, in my opinion, spoiled many business owners. It's made them believe that there are thousands and thousands of potential customers out there for them (which there are) and that they should be able to put their name in front of them for free (maybe not).

I see business owners getting really upset when a social media platform begins to throttle their reach somewhat, stops showing their page to new followers or when it expects them to pay to play.

We've had it good over the last 10 years or so. Maybe too good, in fact. Some have built social media followings in the millions without ever paying a penny to do so. Whilst this is wonderful for them, I suspect that won't always be possible. Social media networks have to make money like everyone else or they won't stick around (which is why you need to get people off them and on to your email list, remember). I predict that, eventually, social media will evolve, and businesses will more frequently have to pay to have their content seen.

I personally have no issue with this. I mean, you wouldn't take a full-page spread out in a newspaper and expect them not to charge you for it. Why would it be free to advertise on social media? Yet this is exactly what so many people do expect. They want their posts to be seen by every single person who follows them and they want it to be free too.

Whilst that may be possible on a very small scale (and milk that for everything it's worth whilst you can, by the way), you will find that a time comes when you want to magnify what you're doing. This is part of the reason it's so important to price yourself correctly; you want to allow some marketing spend so that you can attract more clients into your business, as well as keeping the existing ones returning more frequently (and spending more too, remember?).

Here's a good way to look at advertising, especially in terms of client acquisition. When you're running advertising campaigns anywhere (and we will look at some specific places shortly in Chapter 11), then think of it as buying customers. You're handing over a few marketing pounds and, in exchange, you're getting a customer. Now, some of those customers will be better than others. Some will try you once and never come back, whilst others will go on to be wonderfully loyal customers for as long as you're in business.

As a business owner, you need to know how much on average your customers are worth to you, how much they are spending each time, how regularly they return and how much you can expect them to spend over the course of a lifetime. Most booking software systems will be able to tell you this – and it's crucial for making good business decisions.

Let's just say that you run some reports, and it transpires that your average client spends £75 each time they visit you, they visit three times per year and they remain a client for five years on average, spending a total of £1,125.

Does that make you feel differently about what a client is worth? How much would you gladly pay to acquire a client like that?

Now, of course, that £1,125 won't all be profit, but if you've done your sums correctly, then a good chunk of it will be. So many people run for the hills at the thought of paid advertising, but wouldn't you gladly write cheques for £100 all day long if someone gave you a £1,000 client in return? That's what paid advertising can do for you.

Paid advertising also allows you to crush your competition and dominate your local marketplace. When you can purchase clients, as described, for more money than your competition can afford to, then you win. Your diary will be full, and they simply won't have a look in. They'll be wondering how you do it. There's no secret sauce there; that's just being smart enough to realise that free advertising is only going to get you so far for so long.

When you'll need paid advertising will depend on your business. We had a busy salon with nine diary columns to fill, so it was important to us to get those filled as quickly as we could. If you just have your own column to fill and you work part time, then perhaps you can get by without too many paid adverts.

But why would you want to? One of the great things about paid advertising is that it makes things happen so much quicker. This isn't a book about running paid ads, and it may be possible to get where you want to go without them, but I owe it to you to lay out all the steps we took – and this was an important one for us.

Please note that, in this section, I'm going to tell you the strategies we used, so that you can borrow them and test them for yourself. This isn't a step-by-step guide or a how-to on setting up adverts. I'm afraid that's a little outside of the remit of this book – plus, the interfaces change so frequently that, by the time this book makes it from my fingertips to the printers, then everything could have changed.

Likewise, I'm going to be concentrating on online advertising here. That's not to say there aren't some offline publications you might like to try in due course too. We did have some success with using leaflets in our local area, and you might have great success with a local magazine or newspaper advert.

If you wish, try them. A large part of marketing is trying new things and seeing if they work – and the past isn't the only indicator of whether something will work or not.

It's therefore a good idea to get into the habit of trying new things. Just make sure that you trial them on a small budget – one you can afford to lose if you get zero enquiries (which could happen, I'm afraid).

You also want to ensure that you have a way of tracking where your calls and clicks are coming from. If you do start to run adverts, then make sure you have unique tracking codes or numbers for them so you know if they are working or not. Otherwise, you're operating purely on guesswork or a hunch – and neither are good ways to build a business.

This is one of the great things about online advertising: you get a huge amount of data at your disposal as well as simply being able to test different versions of the same advert. Google makes it really easy to test different headlines, images and advertisement copy to see which combination will work best for you – and all at no additional cost.

I want to take you back to what we did and why we did it.

(As a side note, we didn't get it right the first time. I don't want to sugar-coat everything for you and tell you that you'll get it perfect right away. You won't. We wasted a whole lot of money before we started to get it right. Hopefully, after reading this, you won't make all of the same mistakes that we did.)

The two main places that we advertised online were the Facebook (now Meta) network and on Google and its partner network.

This is a good time to discuss the differences between the two networks. Lots of people ask me where they should advertise: on social media networks or on Google? The thing to grasp here is that they are actually different types of marketing platform, and therefore should be approached differently.

Using Facebook and other social media platforms is interruption-based marketing. That means nobody is out looking for you as such; you're just showing up in their newsfeed, in their stories or wherever. You're hoping that you can make them stop what they are doing and give a little bit of time to you. This is a competitive space, and stopping someone from doing something else is not always easy.

Advertising on Google – so that you show up when people type certain terms or phrases into the search bar (although there are many other types of Google advert too) – is intent-based marketing. That means someone out there is looking, at that very moment in time, for what you're offering. You're not trying to distract them from something else – they are literally asking for help from Google to find you.

Take a moment to consider how different these approaches really are. Think also about how different the end users are. I'd argue that one of them is a warm lead ready to be converted to a client, whereas – whilst the other may get there – it might also take a little work from you to get them over the line. I know which I'd rather have, and that's why we started with the Google Ads platform.

If you're planning on running some adverts, then it's imperative that you know your numbers. You must have an idea of how much you're willing to spend for an enquiry or a booking. If you don't know these numbers, then please do not even think about running ads until you do. Remember that we're here to make a profit, so having a good grasp on this is essential.

This was one of the first areas we messed up. We started running ads for treatments and services that weren't profitable enough to allow for an advertising budget. It's going to be very difficult to run adverts, for example, for lower-priced services (such as lip waxes or spray tans) or for treatments with tight margins (such as nail treatments). We found that it worked much better for our more expensive treatments and experiences – especially those priced at £100 or more.

As the profitability was so much higher with these treatments, we were able to hand some money over to Google and still make a profit. In fact, we gladly handed over lots to them every single month. We ran successful advertising campaigns for spa days, non-surgical facelifts, fat freezing and more. We didn't bother for nail treatments, tanning or any of the day-to-day treatments.

This is another reason why I'd encourage you to offer more high-priced (and high-profit) services if you don't already. You can simply do more with the other money that is then in your business. You can also run advertising campaigns all day long – at a profit – and get so much more exposure to the marketplace than the business down the road, which can't afford to get a look in. More on this later.

The other type of advertising we did on Google was using its display network adverts. You'll most probably have seen these today and every day that you're on the internet. Google has millions of websites (some they own, and some they don't), and it'll be happy to show your ads on these sites. These are typically an image plus a few lines of text, and they can show up in a variety of shapes and sizes, depending on the website.

One of the great things about these is that they are very inexpensive to run, and if you desire to, then you can pay only when people actually click on your advertisement. That means if thousands of people see it, but only one clicks through, then you're only paying the one time. Pretty sweet, when you think about it.

For these advertisements, we ran what are called 'retargeting adverts'. We put a little bit of code on our website called a 'retargeting pixel'. That pixel tells us when someone visits our website. Assuming they don't have some tracking blockers, we are then able to show our adverts to them – and only to those people who have triggered the pixel by clicking on our website.

To see this in action, all you need to do is visit the website of any of the large clothing retailers, and you'll then be followed around the internet by them for the following days. Nike and Adidas are especially good at this, which they do by showing you images of things you almost purchased in an attempt to get you over the line.

So, every month on Google, we would also run adverts – which were only shown to people who had already visited our website – for our monthly LEUEs. The reason for this was that we only wanted to show it to people who already knew us. These were the same people we were originally targeting, remember? The ones whom we wanted coming back more often and spending more money with us. As a result of the adverts only being shown to those who were likely to be a good fit for us, it also kept the price of the adverts lower.

So, by way of a quick recap, the adverts we ran on Google were search-based ads that were shown to anyone who was searching Google locally for our premium offerings and also retargeting adverts for our monthly LEUEs that just went to those who'd already expressed some interest.

On Facebook, we had a slightly different strategy. Again, we were going to run different adverts for different people. The first change was that we didn't run adverts for our main treatments and services at all – not even the more profitable ones. The main reason was that we found it was too expensive to take someone from not being interested in something to being interested enough to purchase. This was much, much easier on Google – where they are telling us they are interested already by searching for it!

(As a quick side note, when advertising on Facebook, you're technically actually advertising on the Meta network, which means you can make the adverts show on Instagram and in other places too. We did do some of this too, even though I'm using the term 'Facebook' to try to keep it less confusing for you).

What we did on Facebook instead was run adverts to two different groups of people. The first group comprised our existing customers: people who had spent money with us already and, sometimes, they were just people who had visited our website or knew whom we were. These were all shown retargeting adverts, as discussed previously, for our LEUE for that month.

The second type of advert we ran on Facebook was sent to people who didn't yet know us. To those people, we didn't show adverts about our treatments or services. We didn't show adverts about our monthly LEUEs, either. We showed them adverts to enter our competition to win a spa day for two people.

This was a much, much easier sale. Trying to get someone who doesn't know you to buy something they aren't looking for can be tricky. Trying to get someone to win a spa day for two in exchange for their email address is far more straightforward.

We also knew by this point that we could nurture people via email from being competition entries to becoming paying customers. All we needed was more email addresses! This was one of the reasons we spent so much time and effort on growing that email list as much as we could. It's such a powerful strategy, and yet one that is, for the most part, underutilised by business owners everywhere.

This section has in no way comprised an exhaustive list of advert types or locations, nor has it set out to. This is simply what we did. Helpfully, it's also where I'd start today if I were doing it again.

Technology moves fast. New advert types and new advertisement platforms will be springing up as I type. As a business owner, it's on you to keep abreast of these and see if you feel they'll be a good fit for your business. Later in this book, when we look more at making the System work for you (in Chapter 14), I'll go deeper into how to figure out where to invest your marketing pounds (or dollars or *insert your local currency here*).

Before I move on – and before I give you a whole host of free ways that you can use to promote your business and your treatments – I want to leave you with a little warning.

Advertising is a little like going to the casino. You could win big. You could also lose everything. There is no guarantee on any return at all, and if you're not good at writing your adverts – or you show them to the wrong people – then it's quite possible that you won't get any return at all.

In my opinion, that's not going to be a reason for everyone not to do it, but it does mean that you should set daily and monthly payment limits so you can control what you're doing – and it also means that, if you're really struggling, perhaps you should just hand everything over to an expert. There are plenty of good people and agencies that will run your adverts for you. Just understand that they aren't cheap (as nobody good is!) and most will be expecting a payment upwards of £500 per month plus the actual cost of the adverts. Again, this illustrates the, ahem, beauty of offering more expensive solutions for your clients – so that all of these things are well within your reach.

If you're a member of our Salonology Gold Club, then you have access to training videos showing you how we did some of this, as well as additional guest-expert training sessions on paid media too.

If you're not a member, you can find out more about it at **www.salonologygoldclub.com**

✓ SOMETHING TO MODEL – Free exposure is only going to get you so far. If you really want to grow – and reach new people – you're going to need to pay to do this at scale. Price yourself high enough and you'll have plenty of profit margin to ensure you can afford to run ads. Just make sure you've done your numbers first.

✘ SOMETHING TO AVOID – Both ad agencies and running paid ads in general can be very expensive. Make sure you have a solid grasp of what you're prepared to spend each month. If you're going to outsource this, then ensure whomever you instruct has tried-and-tested methods and relevant industry results.

CHAPTER 10

FEEDING YOUR SYSTEM

You'll have realised by now that we didn't do things the way that everyone else was doing them. That was intentional. After all, most people were getting results that we wouldn't have been happy with. Most local businesses are surviving and not thriving, so we knew we'd have to do something different if we wanted to have a business that truly served us.

We knew that we just needed to feed our System. We also knew that it was much easier – and far less expensive – to get people into our System and turn them into repeat customers than it was to attract them in the first place.

For us, it was all about getting people's email addresses and getting them entered into our monthly prize draw. In this chapter, I'm going to lay out some of the best ways that we managed to get people into that draw. You might want to test some of these out for yourself too.

You might just notice as well that we tried lots of different things. That was probably one of the things that helped make it a success. We weren't in the habit of trying one thing and then giving up. That wasn't an option. I'd strongly recommend that you get into the habit of trying new stuff too (heck, there are enough ideas contained within these pages) as some of it will work beautifully.

We'll begin with where else we placed our competition entry online. Remember, this competition is our main way of attracting people into our business, so it's important that it's in lots of places. Everywhere you can think of, really.

We had it all over our social media channels, of course. In bios, on cover photos, on our personal pages, in descriptions, in about sections and in headers – pretty much anywhere that we could place a clickable link, as we wanted people to be able to click and enter our competition.

Likewise, we wanted to make it really obvious on our website. There's nothing worse than when you can't find the information you need on a website, and we wanted people to be able to sign up in just a few clicks.

Therefore, we had our website team add the competition to every page of the website. Yup, every single one! We had a WordPress website, so it was actually very easy for them to add a sign-up box into the main template the website used. This ensured it was on all of the pages.

This meant that every time someone read a blog or watched a video on our website, then right after, they'd see the opportunity to win a spa day with us. This was enough to get thousands and thousands over the line and registered for a chance to win.

This was the same for our YouTube channel. For every video we uploaded, we'd include within the video description a link to enter the competition.

We also spoke about the competition offline too. We wanted everyone talking about it, so it was imperative that it was mentioned a lot. If you're going to be in something, then you may as well go all in – and nowhere is that statement more true than in the world of marketing.

Your friends in the offline world these days are QR codes. These are little, square barcodes your phone can read that send the scanner to the website page you desire. They are ideal for driving people to your competition (or, indeed, whichever vehicle you choose to collect email addresses).

The first and most obvious place to have this would be on your reception desk. It's going to be seen there by lots of people and get plenty of exposure. It also becomes a talking point if someone is visiting with their friends. Typically, if one enters, then they all will. You might also want to consider having another QR code there so that people can leave you a Google review too.

You can be as imaginative as you like with where you place these within your salon – and where is best for you will be somewhat unique to your space. The backs of toilet doors can be an underutilised area, as well as being an area viewed with regularity!

How about on the window of your salon to catch the eye of people passing by? How about on an A-board outside? What about having it on your menu or price list too?

You may think this is overkill and that, for some reason, people would be annoyed or irritated in some way by seeing it all the time. We certainly didn't experience this at all. Plus, remember that people need to see something lots of times before they take action. We also wanted the competition to remain at the front of the minds of the clients who had already entered. We wanted them to be excited about it. We wanted them to tell their friends. We really, really wanted them to open that email on the first of every month!

Your consultation form is another great place to mention your competition. You're already asking people for their email address, so why not give yourself the best chance of them agreeing to your marketing communications too? They are far more likely to give their authority for you to contact them if they think they'll win something (or get *something* additional in exchange) than if they think they are just going to get a whole load of unsolicited sales emails.

Consider also anything that your clients will walk away with. Are they given physical appointment cards? Do you give out business cards when you meet people? If so, then both of these can easily have a QR code added, along with a simple, one-line call to action to encourage people to enter the competition.

This is really, really simple stuff. Don't let that put you off, though. It can also be really effective – especially when you take massive action on these things all at once. The more you put into place in your business, the more your results will grow (perhaps exponentially).

There were also a couple of other really cool things that happened once we had all of the parts of this System built and working.

The first was that people were seeing us everywhere. They would be getting emails several times per week. They might see two or three social media posts from us. There was every chance they'd see some of our social media adverts on top of that, and it was the same with our Google adverts (which would show up on all kinds of websites).

Due to the types of adverts we were running, we were able to put our name (and in many cases, our LEUE) right under the noses of the exact people that we wanted to see it. If someone was already on our email list, then they'd see these adverts, and if they weren't, then we'd show them an advert encouraging them to enter our competition.

They believed we were all over the place – and we were. To them, anyway, but importantly, *not to everyone.*

Remember that many of the adverts we were running were only being shown to certain groups of people. Those people would have felt we were spending thousands and thousands on adverts every month, but the reality was that most other people wouldn't have known who we are. We weren't trying to appeal to everyone, so not everyone saw our adverts.

In marketing, this is called 'being omnipresent'. Showing up across a wide range of channels to give the impression that you're simply everywhere. This leads to more brand recognition and more repeat business. It means that you're the first person your client thinks about when considering what you offer. It can also carve you out as an expert or market leader in your field. These are all things that will help your business tremendously.

This was what our System looked like. You're going to want to tweak yours to suit your business and what you offer. To help you even further, I'm going to lay out later in this book (in Chapter 14) some of the things I'd be trying today.

You might be wondering how you can best adapt this to your specific business; after all, everyone's business is a little different, right?

Well, that comes down to knowing your clients and, moreover, knowing how to put the right message in front of them...

✓ **SOMETHING TO MODEL** – Become committed to testing new things. You really never know whether something will work until you try it. What works for one person might not work for another, especially if they are targeting a different type of client. Test it, look at the feedback and then try to improve on it. This cycle continues pretty much forever.

✗ **SOMETHING TO AVOID** – Don't be put off by thinking that there seems to be a lot of things to do. We didn't build our System overnight, it was developed over several years. Even if you only tried one new method per month for a year, you'd have a dozen new ways for people to find you that you don't have right now. That's probably 10 more than your competitors have too.

CHAPTER 11

MARKETING 101

If you've been in our world for any period of time, then you'll have heard me say before that I believe marketing is the number one skill for business owners to master (or at the very least, to learn a bit more about).

This is partly because better marketing, leading to more revenue, can solve pretty much all of the problems that can – and will – happen in your business.

It's also an area so many business owners struggle with, meaning that even a basic understanding of what is happening can lead to exponentially better results for them.

Have you ever had the experience where there's a competitor down the road from you who is always busier than you – even though you know full well that their services and treatments aren't as good?

Not only that but also their decor isn't as nice, their staff aren't as welcoming and they serve nasty supermarket-own-brand instant coffee. Damn.

How can this be?

The answer, almost certainly, is due to them doing a better job of their marketing – which, as it happens, is good news for you, as marketing is also a learnable skill and that means you can learn it too. Just like they did.

Yes, the fact of the matter is that you can be the best stylist in Manchester, the top reiki master in Cleethorpes or even the number one facialist in Timbuktu, but none of that matters one iota if nobody knows you exist.

If you've ever struggled to attract as many folks into your business as you'd like to, then this chapter is for you.

Let's start with the formula for attracting all the clients you'll ever need into your business:

Putting the right messages, in front of the right people, at the right time and using the right channels.

That's it. This is sometimes also spoken of as the 'three Ms of marketing' (that's market, message and media).

We'll begin by working out whom the right people are that we want to attract.

Do you approach your client attraction with the attitude that simply anyone will do? Many salon owners I speak with have an incredibly vague idea of whom they are trying to attract. Something along the lines of 'women under 50 who live in my town'.

But you see, that's just not specific enough to attract anyone. Plus, as you'll remember from my voucher-site story, it also includes a large number of people whom we'd rather not attract at all, thank you very much.

We want to go a little bit deeper than basic demographics here. Age, sex and location are a fine place to start, but how else can we define these dream clients?

The more that we know about these people, the better. This will help us to create the perfect messaging for them. More about that in a moment.

For now, here are some questions for you to ponder. Why not spend 15 minutes or so jotting down some thoughts or ideas, so that you can build up a more colourful picture of these hypothetical guests than you have before?

You might be looking to attract several different types of client, and that's fine, but for this exercise, you'll be best advised to treat each one separately. For example, you may have clients who are broadly interested in anti-ageing, whilst you have another section who are all about looking as glam as possible.

That's fine, but the messages you put out there won't attract both of those people at the same time. Those two client types would need to hear very different messages for them to believe that you're the person or business that can help them.

Remember that the more we know about them, the easier it's going to be to put our message in front of them.

Start by thinking about how you actually help people. Your clients have issues, problems and pain points, and you need to discover exactly what these are. In fact, you need to know them better than they do, wherever possible.

Why is this so important? Well, because we all make buying decisions emotionally. We buy with our emotions, and then we look for logical reasons to justify the purchase.

For example, you might want to treat yourself to a new pair of shoes. You'll make the purchase emotionally – perhaps by thinking how wonderful you'll feel when you slip those Louboutins on – but you'll then justify the purchase logically, with a story about how you deserve it, how you've worked extra hard this month or how you've not had a new pair for ages.

Your clients will make purchase decisions the same way – as we all do – so you need to make sure you're pulling the correct emotional levers.

What's the result that you actually give your clients?

What's the single biggest thing they are struggling with right now?

What's the thing they want more than anything else?

What would happen if they didn't solve their problem?

What feelings or emotions do they have that they'd rather they didn't?

When you start to answer these questions, you'll immediately be a huge leap ahead of the pack. Most businesses don't communicate these types of things with their customers. But then, most businesses don't make any real money either.

Let's say for a moment that you offer lashes in your salon. If you put up posts or adverts that say something along the lines of "A full set of lashes for just £49", then I imagine you'll not get much traction.

Why? Because people don't want a set of lashes. What they actually want is to feel amazing at that school reunion they have coming up. Or they want to show their ex what they are missing. Or they want to make their nemesis jealous. You get the idea.

Think about what it is that your clients really want, and then start to craft your marketing messages around that.

Once you have a much better idea of whom it is you're trying to attract into your business (based, by and large, on how you actually help people), you'll then want to consider the type of message they need to hear.

Have you ever read a post on social media and then thought to yourself that it was as if that post were talking directly to you and nobody else? Almost as if the author of the post knew you better than you know yourself? Well, that's the type of messaging we're talking about here.

It's the type of messaging that actually moves people to take some action, whatever that action may be.

Grabbing a blank piece of paper for a good old-fashioned brainstorming session might be a good idea at this point. Scribble down as many ideas as you can in terms of the following:

» All the different features and benefits of your treatments or services (think about what the treatment does for them, why they should care and tie that in to the emotional reasons)

» All the problems and potential problems that you or your treatments or services solve

» All the great reasons as to why someone would go ahead and make a booking with your business

» All the possible objections that they might have to moving forwards with you

Everything that you just listed can become a potential pillar of content for your business. You might turn any one of these into a social media post, a video, an email, a blog article, an editorial piece or even an actual paid advertisement.

These won't account for everything you put out into the world, of course, but I'm certainly going to encourage you to at least try some written in this manner. It's a big switch going from talking about you to talking about them. It's also one worth getting better at.

The final part of the three-Ms puzzle is the media (or channel) by which you get your messages in front of the right people.

You can have the best message in the world, but if you're showing it to the wrong folks, then your hard work and efforts have all been wasted.

In my previous book (*The Customer Is Always Right; and 7.5 Other Outdated Myths Which Are Destroying Your Beauty Salon Business*), I used the example that if you were trying to attract a 21-year-old for her lash-extension treatments, then perhaps using Instagram or TikTok would be a good option. Conversely, if it was that client's mum you were trying to attract for anti-ageing facials, then maybe using Facebook would be a better method. Finally, if you were looking to attract her gran (or perhaps her great-gran) for exfoliating pedicure treatments, then perhaps a leaflet through the door or index cards in the local shop window would be the most suitable route.

Your message needs to be put in front of the right people. Therefore, you need to work out where you think they might be hanging out. This is why it's so crucial to understand as much as you can about whom you're really trying to reach.

Where are your clients hanging out? Are they on Facebook? If so, which groups are they in?

Are they easier to communicate with offline? If so, what publications do they read? Where do they frequent? What do they enjoy doing in their spare time?

Let's say that you specialise in vegan anti-ageing treatments and you only use certified cruelty-free products.

Where would the people who would potentially be a good fit for you be hiding?

Let's start with the online side of things. Are there certain local Facebook groups they might be part of? Are there certain YouTube channels or Instagram accounts that they might follow? What blogs might they be reading?

When we know this (and, again, much of it will be trial and error to begin with), we can think of ways that we can get in front of them. For example, we might join the relevant Facebook groups and comment where appropriate, use the hashtags we think they'll see, or even approach other online content creators to see if we can contribute to their website or channels.

With time and regularity, people will start to see your name more and more and, hopefully, associate it with creating useful content. They will also more than likely start to see you as the expert in your field. Imagine if the right people considered you to be the go-to expert in your field for what you help your clients with. Think what that could do for your business!

Let's also consider the offline side of things too. Where is your TC spending their spare time? What other pursuits do they enjoy? Who else already has a relationship with them?

So, again, for our vegan anti-ageing specialist, they might want to see which other vegan businesses their client frequents. This could be a vegan hair salon, a café or even a clothing brand. Maybe there's an annual vegan exhibition or event in the town, or maybe there's a new vegan restaurant opening locally.

One really smart shortcut you can take is by considering this: there are other businesses in your locale who already have a relationship with your dream client. If these are non-competing businesses, then you owe it to yourself to get in front of them and see if you can create some form of win-win-win situation. That is, a situation where the client wins, the other business wins and you also win.

This might be a simple agreement with another company to recommend one another. It might be that you club together for some form of event. Perhaps you can even get them to email their client base to tell their clients about you.

These types of opportunity seldom come along by themselves. You need to be proactive and take the first steps. You might think that sounds like a lot of hard work, but before you discount it immediately, just take a moment to ponder the impact it could have on your business if multiple other businesses were all recommending you as their tried-and-tested supplier of whatever it is you do.

Let's loop back to the little formula I explained at the top of this chapter for attracting dream clients: putting the right messages, in front of the right people, at the right time and using the right channels.

We've looked at how to craft the right message for the exact person and even the ways to ensure they see it. So, how do we know when the right time is?

Here's where so many fall down. They pop one social media post up, and they expect the whole world to drop what they are doing and form an orderly queue outside their salon. You probably don't need me to tell you that, in reality, it's not going to happen.

I've already mentioned that people, on average, need to see you and your content 20 times before they are comfortable enough to move forwards with you.[8] Remember also that they typically need to see your offer seven times! Are you giving people enough opportunities to see you? Or are you giving up after nothing more than dipping your toe in the water?

Let's say you're sitting at home and mindlessly scrolling through Facebook when you see an advert for a new salon in your area. Be honest now, how likely are you to just dive in and book an appointment with them?

I'd argue *very* unlikely! Yet this is exactly what salon owners are complaining about when they say that people aren't responding to them or their posts. Maybe they just don't know you well enough yet. Maybe they don't understand how you can help them with their problem. Maybe they had a facial last week and don't need another right now. Maybe they didn't even see the post.

If you're only emailing your clients once in a blue moon or you're only posting to social media once per week, then that's likely to be a big part of the problem. We want to be putting out lots of marketing messages so that we'll find the right people at the right time. We must be giving our clients plenty of opportunities to find out what we're all about. The more often we go fishing, the more fish we're likely to catch!

So many make the assumption that people already know about us and what we do, when the reality is that many don't.

This is why it's so important to ensure we're giving clients the chance to get to know, like and trust us, as those KLTFs are the keys to turning a stranger into a client and then into a salon ambassador who brings all their friends in with them. It's also what we're going to cover next.

✓ **SOMETHING TO MODEL** – Marketing is the number one skill that business owners need to get better at. There is a direct link between the quality of your marketing, the quality of your clients and how much money is in your till at the end of the month. It's a learnable skill, so take the time to learn it.

✗ **SOMETHING TO AVOID** – Don't leave people finding you to chance. Make it impossible for them to miss you! Just being good at what you do isn't enough – if nobody has heard of you, then you won't be in business for very long.

CHAPTER 12

THE KNOW, LIKE AND TRUST FACTORS (KLTFs)

The way that your clients will progress through your System is via your KLTFs. KLTF stands for 'know, like and trust factor', and these factors are the various ones that will help your clients to get to know you and your business better, make them more comfortable with you and, ultimately, to ascend them from being mildly aware of you to becoming a regular client (hopefully!) and then a rabid fan.

Bob Burg, author of the marvellous book *The Go-Giver*, observes, "All things being equal, people will do business with, and refer business to, those people they know, like, and trust."[9]

That's what we want: people so in love with you and your business that they visit regularly, take everything you offer them and tell all of their friends about you.

This doesn't happen overnight. You can assume that most people will be fairly cynical to begin with, and it'll take a little time to build up those levels of trust.

It's 20 touches, remember?

Whilst we've referenced some of these KLTFs elsewhere, I felt it would be useful to categorise them together here also.

Think of you and your dream TC standing on either side of a room. Every time they feel they know a little bit more about you, and they like what they hear, then they take a baby step forwards.

They continue to do this until they've taken, on average, 20 of those steps, and then they are nose to nose with you! This is the point at which the magic happens, and they feel comfortable enough to listen to your recommendations, book a consultation or proceed in some way.

So, how do we help them to make these steps? With your KLTFs.

We want our clients to know us, then like us and then, finally, trust us enough to look after them within our business. Not only will this ascend our clients through the System more quickly, but it'll also result in better relationships with our clients, fewer refunds and more referrals. You don't need me to tell you that these are all good things for your business.

We'll begin with know. How can we best get to know our clients or, rather, let *them* get to know *us*?

This begins with understanding exactly whom it is that we are trying to attract into our business. We don't want everyone; we just want those who are going to be a good fit. The more you know about them, the easier it will be to find them (or rather the easier it will be for them to magically discover you).

Think about where your target audience is likely to already be hanging out. What publications might they read? What radio stations do they listen to? What Facebook groups do they congregate in? What do they like to do in their spare time? Do they have children, and if so, then what schools do those children attend? You've got to go deeper than simply finding out how old they are and which town they live in.

A brilliant shortcut here – especially if you're looking to attract new clients – is to consider who already has an existing relationship with your clients. There is someone somewhere who is an absolute trusted authority to the exact people you're trying to find. If you could find a way to link up with them, then it could open a serious amount of doors for you.

If you're a vegan salon, for example, then there are probably several vegan cafés and restaurants that already have such relationships. If you offer sports massage, then perhaps personal trainers would be worth approaching. Think outside the box and don't expect everyone you approach to jump at the chance of working with you. However, the good news is that you don't need many of these relationships for it to have a really positive impact for you.

When we owned our spa, we contacted all of the other local hotels that didn't have spa facilities and we offered them a way of selling spa services to their clients. That was send them to us! It was a win-win situation, and everyone got what they wanted. The hotel guest could have a relaxing treatment from a trusted partner; the hotel managed to secure their booking when maybe they wouldn't have otherwise – and have a happy patron; and we got a new client to look after. Everyone won.

We also made connections and friendships with local journalists. You'd be amazed at how easy it can be to get publicity when you know the right people. Make connections, invite them in for an experience and give them something to write about!

We ended up not only being featured in the local press but also in the *Daily Mirror* and *Professional Beauty* magazine, and we appeared on both BBC3 and Channel Four! We didn't pay a penny for any of that exposure either. We just offered up a few experiences and had the audacity to reach out and contact them, rather than waiting for them to contact us. It's not rocket science; it's just putting yourself in front of the right people who have the right connections.

Doing something out of the ordinary is also a wonderful way to get noticed. Do something amazing for charity. Or for your local food bank. Or a local women's refuge. Or whatever means something to you.

The press can pick up on that sort of thing, and people love it when folks do nice things.

We also found that our monthly prize draw was a brilliant way to garner the attention of people who hadn't heard of us until that point. It seems that everyone likes the chance to be a winner.

So let's now assume people have heard of you or your business. How do we get them to like us?

Well, for me, again, it all begins with the concept of pulling back the curtain and letting people in a little more.

Perhaps you already do this to a degree in your business or perhaps you're a part of another group of folks who simply want to keep their personal life personal and their business life for business.

Whilst I completely understand that everyone has a different comfort level regarding the extent of what they are happy to share online, I'd encourage you to push this a little more than you perhaps do currently. There are many who simply never post any indication whatsoever about who the face is behind their logo. In my opinion, this is a seriously missed opportunity.

Not doing this doesn't mean that you won't ever get any clients; it just means that it'll take you much longer to ascend people through your System. If you're fine with that, then great! If you'd like to speed up the process somewhat, then this is a good place to begin.

People buy people. They don't buy logos. We can't relate to a logo in the same way that we can to a face and a voice. We can't recognise or remember a logo as well as a face either. Here's something important to note in such a highly competitive arena: one of the best ways to become both more memorable and more likeable is by displaying more of you and that pretty little face of yours.

Do a little search on Instagram for other businesses in your area that offer similar services to you. There will most likely be plenty to choose from. Scroll through their profiles and look at the images and videos posted.

Most likely, many of them will be indistinguishable from the others. They'll have image after image that are 'before and after' shots. I'm not saying photos of your work aren't important – they have a place, for sure – but lots of other things are important also.

I predict that many of these profiles will have no mention at all of who is behind the brand. No image. No story. Nothing.

Somebody trusting you with their beauty, hair or aesthetic requirements is a big deal. They want to know a little more about you before they are just going to hand over the money blindly. It's the same as you would be if you were to look for a new salon. Make it easy for them so that they don't keep scrolling on to the next one.

Assuming that you're a local business owner, then the vast majority of the time, you will be a huge part of the business – and a huge part of what attracts clients to want to work with you and your team, even if you're not the one who is actually delivering the treatments.

So, put yourself out there a little more. Include more images of you and your team. Use the stories features of social media platforms to show people what happens behind the scenes. Let them know how you spend your days off. If you have a dog, then include pictures of little Mr Wooferson from time to time.

Be real, be authentic and inject as much personality in there as you possibly can. Embrace your quirks. Not only will many people love you for it but it'll also make you memorable, and that's half of the battle in a world where everyone is so easily distracted.

Consider what it is that you wish to be known for and play to that. You don't need to be famous to millions of people, but becoming famous to a few (that is, the locals in your area who desire what you do) is where the money is.

Look, people are nosey. They want to know what is going on in your life. In fact, when you think about it, that's the entire premise of social media, no less! People having a good nose at what others are doing.

Something else that very few businesses pay attention to – and something else that really helps to allow people to get to know you, like you and, ultimately, trust you more quickly – is storytelling.

I touched on this earlier (in Chapters 6 and 8), but now I want to lay out a few specific things that you can do to help people along on their journey with you.

One of the wonderful things about stories is that the reader's guard is down. They aren't expecting to be sold to, which means that your message is more likely to get across.

(To be clear, I don't mean the feature on Facebook and Instagram with the same name – I'm talking about telling stories in your marketing, be it via video, written blogs, emails or even long-form social media posts).

Lots of people overcomplicate the idea of storytelling, but I hope that you'll embrace it and start weaving more stories into the content you create for your clients. Your stories will help you to do much of the heavy lifting in bringing your clients closer to you – all the time, without sounding salesy or in any way pushy or sleazy.

Can you think of a better way to help our clients to know, like and trust us than with simple storytelling? I can't, and even more so when some of these stories are pulling back the curtain so that people can actually connect with us. You see, as human beings, we all crave that connection with other people. Stories help to facilitate this.

We are also drawn to others who share the same values, thoughts and opinions as us. Again, stories allow us to share insight into these potential areas of common ground.

If you happen to have a rare breed of dog and you share a story online about how little Monty won his first rosette at a dog show, then I promise you that the other dog lovers who read it will feel closer to you. Even if dogs are nothing to do with your business.

It all helps to deepen the bond between you and your clients. And don't forget what bonds build. (Businesses, in case you had indeed forgotten.)

We liked using stories in our email content as they are a wonderful way to disguise the second reason we had for sending it. Reason one was to deepen the bonds, and reason two was usually to offer an appointment in our diaries. I'd strongly recommend that you start there also. Don't expect a reply to every single one you send out, but likewise, don't think that people aren't reading them. They will be.

You can wrap a story around pretty much anything you like – they can be personal, they can be work related, they can be about your team, they can be about local news or they can be about little Monty the Dachshund.

Don't overthink it; just start firing some out. With a little time (because not everyone does this, can you believe?), people will start to love you for it.

There are also a few stories that everyone should tell. One of those is the story of why you do what you do. I'd strongly recommend having this on your website somewhere. This should be an emotion-led story about how you got into the business and why you're so damned passionate about what you do for people.

Likewise, you need a story all about who you help and how you help them. This should be one of those stories where your dream client reads it and thinks, *Hey, she's talking about me here!* Again, your website would be a good place to put this.

So let's assume that people are now aware of who you are, and they even like you. Yay! It's the final part of the jigsaw, the trust element, which will either get them over the line or have them running for the hills.

Have you ever wandered out of a shop, laden with bags, and remarked to your other half, "Wasn't that assistant lovely?"

Likewise, have you ever run a mile from a car dealership or an estate agent thinking, *I wouldn't buy anything from them!*?

We all have, and it's because of the perceived level of trust (or lack thereof). Buying something from someone you don't know (outside very small or insignificant purchases) is uncommon, buying from someone you don't like is even rarer and buying from someone you don't trust seldom happens.

Case studies and testimonials are a great way to build trust. These should be sprinkled on everything you do and woven into your website and social media content. 'Before and after' photos are great, but case studies are much better.

You want to evoke emotion here, which is why case studies work so well. They are also a form of storytelling, which we also want to use as much as we can. The formula I recommend using for a powerful case study is as follows: how the client felt before they met you (and specifically, the pain they were in), what you prescribed for them and how that happened, and finally, how they feel now. This will really resonate with others experiencing the same.

Reviews are also great for building trust, and a staggering 87% of people are believed to check Google reviews before making a purchasing decision.[10] That's an incredible number of people. You should have a system for collecting these reviews and then sharing them like clockwork. You want to have such a ridiculous number that people couldn't possibly doubt them.

Don't worry about collecting them anywhere outside Google – that's where you want them. It'll help your Google ranking by having them, and ultimately, who *doesn't* use Google?

Something in a similar vein to testimonials and reviews is social proof.

This is something that has become more and more important in recent years for businesses of all types, including yours. Social proof, a coin termed by Robert Cialdini, is where people are driven to copy the actions of others in a situation in which they don't know how to act.

You've no doubt heard the idea that people are like sheep, and social proof plays to this. It is a type of conformity, or herd behaviour, in which people mimic the actions of others. This is one of the reasons why testimonials and case studies are important to our businesses. However, social proof takes it one step further.

In the digital age we live in, people are more sceptical than ever. They know how easy it would be for you to make up or distort a testimonial piece if you really wanted to. What isn't so easy, however, is manipulating a post or discussion on social media for which tens of people all weigh in to back up the claims made.

Let me give you an example. In our salon, we'd often (and I do mean often) post about our LEUEs. One month, we might put up a post asking who'd enjoyed it this month. What was the reason for this? We wanted to garner lots of comments from happy people – comments that might then be seen by some of those sitting on the fence about going ahead and booking.

Put yourself in the position of the fence sitter. You've seen something on Facebook. You're kind of interested, but you've not been to that salon before, so you're not sure. Then you see this new post and can read the comments underneath by half a dozen or so other people who all said how much they loved it. Would that be enough to get you over the line? It would for lots of people, and that's how social proof works.

First, we know someone; then, we decide if we like them; and finally, we decide if we trust them. In that order, over time, based on the information we know. We can help people along this little journey with the content we're putting in front of them.

These factors are always at play in both bringing people into your world initially and ascending them from being someone who simply knows you to someone who is a raving-bonkers cheerleader for you.

They also help to ascend people in your System to where the real money lies.

✓ **SOMETHING TO MODEL** – People want to do business with people that they know, like and trust. Make sure that your dream clients know about you, like you and trust you!

✘ **SOMETHING TO AVOID** – People don't want to do business with a logo; they want to do business with people. Don't hide behind your logo, and be brave enough to put your name and your face in front of your clients – even if you've a big team and even if you don't deliver the services or treatments yourself. This is how relationships and bonds are built. And bonds build businesses, as Hollie always says (and she's right).

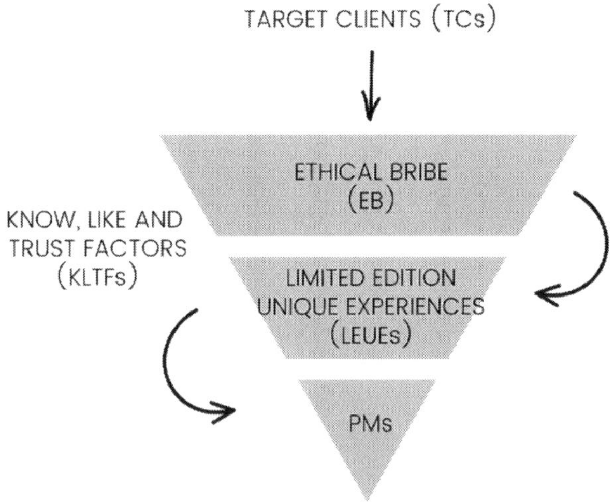

Your System is almost complete

CHAPTER 13

THE PROFIT MAXIMISERS (PMs)

It was 2017, and we had another problem in our day spa and salon.

It was a problem that I've since learned many salon owners also unwittingly have. It's also a problem that, when solved, can completely change the game. It certainly did for us.

You'll hopefully remember earlier in the book (in Chapter 4) when I spoke of Jay Abraham's three ways to grow a business. In case you need a little reminder, those three ways are to increase the number of clients you serve, increase the frequency of visits and increase the average transaction size per visit.[11] That's it.

The purpose of our monthly LEUEs was to increase the frequency with which people visited us. It worked too.

You see, most business owners are always looking to attract new clients. Now, whilst this is important, as some will leave your world over time, it's also important to realise something else:

It costs six times more money to attract a new client as it does an existing one.[12]

Read that again.

What that means is that those you have an existing relationship with are the low-hanging fruit here. They are the ones who should get the majority of your attention in bringing them back into your business. This is precisely why our LEUEs existed: to give people a brilliant reason to return – and to return with regularity.

Why is it so much easier – and cheaper – to attract these folks back?

Because they know, like and trust you, of course! Yay for that KLTF bringing folks back time and time again – that's coupled with delivering exceptional treatments and offering a top level of service, of course, but I'm going to assume that you've already got that side of things covered!

So we had already dramatically improved the frequency of our clients' visits, but this left the one remaining piece of the puzzle: the average transaction value.

Now our day spa and salon was by no means the least expensive in town, but likewise, it wasn't super exclusive either.

So we needed a way that we could really bump up the numbers. We realised that our treatment menu was a little swollen; there were too many inexpensive treatments and not enough really expensive ones.

By 'really expensive' I mean that, outside a few packages, there were very few treatments costing more than £100 and fewer still as you creep up past £250.

We knew that this was an area we needed to look at. The fact of the matter is that there will always be people who will spend more money with you if you give them the opportunity to. Likewise, there are also people who will always take the luxury, the VIP or the extended versions of your offerings. Always. It's just how some people are wired. (You are offering those on your menu, right?)

There are some treatments and services that, on average, sell for around £50. There are others that are closer to double that, which can be delivered in the same amount of time and with similar costs. Which do you think it makes more sense to concentrate your promotional efforts on? For me, I would want to focus on the ones that make the most profit.

This isn't because I'm some elitist, capitalist pig, by the way, but it's because I'm a business owner, and without profit, there is no business. It's as simple as that.

Sometimes, we have to try to remove some of the emotions in our business decision-making, as hard as that can be. It breaks my heart when I see some who are slaves to their respective business, barely making ends meet, all because they think they have to focus on some of the more traditional salon offerings (which also often make the least profit).

You owe it to yourself, your future self, your family and your business to concentrate on where the money is. It's that same money that will allow you to pay yourself a wage, pay your staff better than average wages, offer a wonderful client experience, invest in your marketing and, who knows, maybe you'll even have enough money left for a few nice holidays every year? Wouldn't that be neat?

It's all possible, but it's much harder if you don't know your numbers or if you're concentrating on services that don't make enough profit. After reading this chapter, go back and run your numbers if you didn't do it before. Those numbers won't lie to you, even if you will lie to yourself!

Now I'm not saying that you need to change your entire menu. I'm not saying don't do the treatments that you love (provided they make you a level of profit you're happy with), but I am saying that, if you want to earn more money – and take more of it home with you – you'll want to find yourself one or more profit maximisers. (PMs)

Perhaps these will be delivered by you, or perhaps they'll be delivered by your team if you have one. Some will require more training than others. Some might require more advanced qualifications. Some will definitely require an investment in some equipment. The good news is that there is something for everyone here; you just need to research the area yourself to find a good fit for you.

(One side note of caution here: we're not looking simply for longer versions of what you already offer. This isn't about selling an eight-hour package, rather it's about selling eight one-hour sessions. We're looking for something that has a higher level of profit *per hour.*)

Some treatments that may be a good fit for you could be semi-permanent make-up, microblading, scalp micropigmentation, fat dissolving, chemical peels, high-end bespoke facials, microdermabrasion, laser hair removal, dermaplaning – and countless more that have probably already surfaced in the time that it took me to write this book!

Here's a top tip to ensure that any PM you look to introduce will not only fit into the ethos of your salon but also ensure a hungry market of buyers is ready and waiting:

Choose something that solves the problem you know your clients have.

Perhaps you already go some way to solving that problem with some of your other offerings. Could you now offer something even more complete?

So, for waxing salons, this could mean bringing in laser hair removal to accompany it, for example. After all, you'll have a long list of people who already trust you with their hair removal needs and perhaps some of them would like to switch to laser if encouraged by a trusted source (that's you). Some won't, and that's fine. But I'll bet that some would, if offered the chance.

You'll want to assess the options to see what works best for you.

We decided to invest in a piece of technology that would allow us to offer a number of higher-priced treatments. The two main ones we focused on were fat freezing and high-intensity, focused ultrasound (HIFU) (basically, the closest you can get to a face lift without going under the knife).

We still offered our usual menu of services. We still offered our monthly LEUEs. But we also now offered these much more expensive treatments too.

The fat freezing was both easy to sell and also very profitable. After taking into consideration the costs of purchasing the machinery (this was no lighthearted investment either; little Maverick the dog's inheritance took a big hit), it was still very profitable indeed.

It was also easy to sell; there are plenty of people out there who want to lose some weight but don't have the time or inclination to hit the gym for months on end. This was especially true in Bournemouth, a somewhat pretentious town where people like to spend time on the beach and generally strutting around.

The fat freezing also created repeat customers of its own; people would be happy with the results on their tummy and then want their thighs done. Even their other halves would come in for treatments!

We could sell a treatment for one area for £150 or more, and it would cost mere pennies to deliver the treatment. Even after all of the running costs of the business and the cost of a therapist, it was still massively profitable.

The HIFU treatment took this to the next level again. It cost around £35 to deliver one treatment, plus it required a full consultation, patch test and all that jazz.

But what was the upside? We could offer a full face treatment – which gave amazing results – for up to £1,500. Many salons don't take that in a week or more – and yet there we were doing that in one 90-minute session.

Now, of course, not everyone wants a £1,500 treatment! But the point is that some people do – and it's our job as marketers to find those people and turn them into believers! That is much easier, of course, when we already have a relationship with them and when they know, like and trust us.

The KLTFs, plus the nurturing emails to our huge database and our 10,000+ Facebook followers, meant that we were able to create massive demand – in spite of the price tag that might make some baulk – from the word go.

You might not have those same advantages that we had, and we were based in an affluent area, but that's why I've laid it all out for you within these pages. Go through everything step by step, and it'll all become easier and easier with time and experience.

This was a total game changer for us, which is why it's included here. Being able to bring large sums of money into the business is essential for growth. It allows you to do so many other things much better.

It meant that we could run adverts – lots and lots of paid adverts – partly because the money in our business meant that we could afford to outspend all of our competition and still make a profit. When you can do that, you win the game.

We invested tens of thousands of pounds into putting our PMs into place. I fully appreciate that you might not be in a position to do that, and I also appreciate that many don't like to take on business debt.

If that's you, then don't start there. Start with a less expensive piece of technology or a training course that allows you or your team to deliver treatments that are more profitable than those you currently offer. You can always level up again down the line when you have more money in your business.

Heck, you could even buy a preloved machine if you wanted to. One of our Salonology team members did just that in her salon, and she paid for the whole thing outright in just a few short weeks. Not years, not months – weeks!

It's easy to think, *I couldn't do that*, but it's more profitable to ask yourself, *How can I make that happen for me?*

The simple fact of the matter is that serving fewer people at a much higher level will do wonders for your profit level. You don't need to stop offering anything that you don't want to, but you do owe it to yourself to at least explore some of the options available to you. Don't miss this important part of your System; it could be the one that changes it all for you.

✓ **SOMETHING TO MODEL** – Never underestimate how much people will spend to move away from their pain points. There are people who will happily and readily spend 10 times the amount they pay you now – if you offer them the correct solution.

✘ **SOMETHING TO AVOID** – Never confuse your own needs, wants or desires with those of your clients. Just because you might never dream of investing £1,000 into your skincare journey, for example, it doesn't mean that nobody else would.

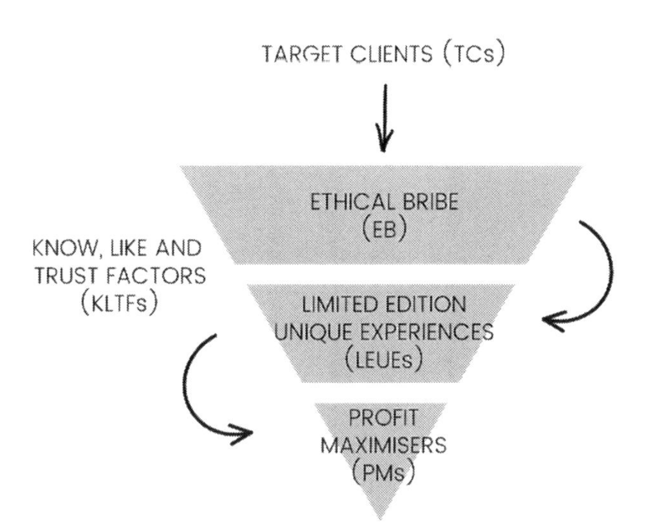

Ta da! Your finished System!

CHAPTER 14

WHAT WILL YOUR SYSTEM LOOK LIKE?

So, that is our System. It didn't look like that on day one – and we certainly didn't get it all in place right away. But after more than a decade of some trial and mostly error, this was more of less the bones of it.

You'll want to adopt this for yourself; there are some variables within the System – different ways that you can pull people into your world.

But the core fundamentals remain the same:

» Find something that attracts people into your world so that you can communicate with them and nurture them (your lead magnet; ours was the monthly competition)

» Get them to the point where they can't resist coming to your business (using your irresistible LEUEs)

» Continue to build your relationship so that you become their absolute first choice (via your KLTFs)

» Ascend them through your System all the way to where the real gold lies (your PMs)

Simple, right?

Since creating our own System, certain things have developed that we'd certainly be including in our arsenal if we still owned our salon today.

This is by no means an exhaustive list – and, indeed, it's likely also to evolve with time. The key is trying out some of these and seeing what works for you, as well as working out what your dream clients respond to.

Remember that your dream TC will probably look a little different to ours. What they respond to will be different. What resonates with them will be different. It's on you to know so much about them that you'll know what they'll love even better than they do. This will come with testing different things and paying attention to your results. Test, adjust, repeat.

Whilst email would undoubtedly still be a huge part of our strategy (because you own the data, and I've still never found a better way to build a relationship with people and take them from having never heard of you to seeing you as the trusted authority), there is another area that we would certainly double down on today. That area is video.

Video has exploded over the last decade or so. Most of us watch lots of videos every single day. The statistics on this are mind boggling. Heck, some people probably watch hundreds of videos per day, given the thirst for bite-sized content that is created for today's easily distracted society. At the time of writing this, the worldwide average is watching 84 minutes of video per person every day![13] That's a crazy number, and I suspect it'll continue to rise.

Video comes in a variety of formats: long form, short form, reels, lives, stories and even boomerangs.

Which formats are the best will vary from platform to platform and will depend on both the current algorithmic trends and what your TCs enjoy consuming. Again, this is for you to test.

I know it's easy to shy away from video. I know that you might hate recording video and putting yourself out there. You're not alone. It's one of the most common things I hear. If that's you, then try to find another way you can utilise video. Get one of your team in front of the camera occasionally. Shoot videos that don't require you speaking into the camera every time. Try voiceovers. Mix it up a little.

But that said, I would encourage you to step in front of the camera at least occasionally too. You want people to see your face. You want to build the bonds that will help take your business to the next level. You want to be seen as the go-to authority in the space and the person whom everyone wants to work with.

All of this, and so much more, is far more easily achieved when you harness the power of video. Your videos don't need to be professionally edited, and you don't need any fancy kit. The smart phone in your pocket is all the equipment you need.

A final couple of words of note regarding video. Don't worry about how you sound. I've yet to meet anyone who has said to me, "I love how I sound on video." It just doesn't happen. Yes, you sound a little different – but not to anyone else. You always sound like that to them. It's only to you that you sound different on playback. Don't let this hold you back, as the rewards are plentiful when you embrace it.

Another area that has really grown since implementing our System is the Google Business Profile (formerly known as Google My Business). Google, of course, has always been important to business. This was exactly why we used to invest heavily in Google Ads every month – notably, to drive entries both to our monthly prize draw and to our PM items too.

However, you don't have to pay to play with Google, and everyone must ensure that their free profile is also kept up to date as a bare minimum. After all, who *isn't* using Google as a search engine?

Doing what you can to show up near the top of the search results when people are looking for what you do is a smart strategy. You don't need me to tell you that. This isn't a book about search engine optimisation (SEO), and indeed, we simply cut that corner altogether by paying Google to ensure we ranked well. But that said, some of the essential (and free-to-implement) basics are worth your while doing. Perhaps even doing right away if you're not doing them already.

The Google algorithm is a complex one. There are estimated to be over 200 different factors that Google takes into consideration when it decides the results to display each time someone searches.[14] Google has never said what these factors are or what weight is given to each of them. It's a closely guarded secret, and most suspected that it changes over time too.

Here are three simple things you can do, after claiming your listing, which will help you in your efforts to rank for your locality. First of all, you need to make sure that your listing is all filled out correctly. And I do mean all of it. Each and every single box that allows text in is an opportunity for Google – and then your potential clients – to find you.

The more that you complete – including, for example, adding your entire menu directly into Google – then the more you'll be shown and the more likely it is you'll be shown closer to the top (which is where you want to be, of course).

Next up, let's add some photos. Google loves them and will reward you for adding them, and yet it's something very few listings have. Your goal here is to add at least 100. This seems to trigger something within your listing that means it gets extra exposure (shout out to John MacLeod of Green Shoot Marketing for that little tip).

You can add them all in one sitting, directly from your phone, or you can drip feed them every day if you prefer. What I've tended to do for our coaching business is upload one per day once we got over the magical 100 photos.

I also changed the file name of the image before uploading it, and also added tags to it too, just because this gives Google two more opportunities to find the image (and thus shows us in the search results) for frankly very little effort on my part.

The third and final thing I recommend is getting as many reviews as humanly possible. Not only do they represent excellent – and essential – social proof (remember that?) but also Google loves them just as much as your future clients will.

Think about it: if you're looking to book a service – literally any service you can think of – are you going to choose the one that has 25 glowing reviews or the one without any? Reports show that up to 97% of people believe that reviews influence their buying decisions, and the vast majority of people turn to Google to read those reviews.[15] Make sure there is something there for people to find when they go looking.

You simply cannot have too many, and you should make the collection of Google reviews a part of the journey that every one of your clients goes through. Automate this as much as possible, and make it simple for people to do it.

Something else that has sprung into the spotlight over recent years is WhatsApp. Again, it seems as though pretty much everyone uses it now. WhatsApp For Business – which has more than 50 million worldwide users[16] and is free to use – can be utilised in much the same way that we used email. In fact, you could even use it in addition to email.

You can broadcast messages, build audiences, accelerate your sales and even use it to deal with your customer service enquiries, should you wish. All for free.

More and more businesses are utilising this – and it's worthy of your attention too. WhatsApp can certainly be leveraged as a KLTF to help cement those relationships and deepen your bonds with your clients.

You can even use it to confirm your appointments, provide aftercare, and request feedback and Google reviews afterwards.

Perhaps you prefer using SMS? Great, do those. In fact, why not double your chances of reaching people and do both?

The final thing I want you to really think about when you unleash your System on the world is that your personality and your uniqueness are your superpowers. This goes for both you as an individual (assuming you're the face of the business) and the physical business itself.

Competition is rife across the board, and the more you can do to stand out and be memorable in a sea of lookalikes, the better.

Be known for something. Become the go-to person for whatever it is you do. Specialise as much as you can. Be different.

It's these things that will help to ensure that your business is talked about as well as giving your clients an amazing reason to keep coming back time and time again – and invite their friends too.

If you can position yourself in a category of one (that is, there is nobody else competing for the precise space you're in), then amazing things can happen. In our day spa and salon, we had the opportunity to expand into an adjacent empty space. Hollie immediately saw the opportunity for a private lounge space – something that nobody else in our area had.

Soon, we were the go-to private hire for groups of hens looking to celebrate as only hens do. Given that Bournemouth is one of the UK's most popular destinations for hen celebrations, you don't need me to tell you that this was a huge success for us.

Adding this as yet another PM, we were able to enjoy takings in the thousands for just one afternoon of private pampering. That's the power of being different.

✓ **SOMETHING TO MODEL** – Take this System and make it your own. What's working right now will change regularly, and so your version will evolve over time – just as ours did. Play to your own strengths too, and exploit your own unique talents as much as you can.

✗ **SOMETHING TO AVOID** – Don't put this book down and forget about it. Take action – now! Even taking a baby step in the right direction beats doing nothing. Don't become another victim of procrastination.

YOUR NEXT STEPS

So, there it is.

My System laid out bare for you to mimic, adapt and implement into your business.

May I let you in on a little secret? I mean, I know that you're one of the special ones. After all, you've made it to the end of this book, and that's something that only a very small percentage of people who start a book actually achieve.

Of those who actually finish a book, how many take action on what they've read? Again, a very small number, I'm sure of that.

I'm the same. I've read hundreds of books that I've then done nothing with – even ones I've enjoyed reading. Guess what results I then achieved as a result of implementing nothing that I'd learned?

That's right: none whatsoever.

I don't want that for you. I know you've not come this far only to come this far. You want that success for you and your business, and quite frankly, you want it yesterday. I admire that fire in your belly!

From here, you've got two choices. Option one is to go ahead and get it all implemented yourself. Go back to Chapter 1 and, piece by piece, put it all together in your business. I know that if you do, with a little time and testing, you'll enjoy some great results.

Option two is to get our help piecing all of this together. We've already recorded full video training guides with step-by-step instructions for many of the parts of the System. We've also got hundreds of salon owners who are already implementing their Systems into their businesses. Not only that but they are also sharing what's working with one another too, as well as getting personal help from Hollie and me.

All of this is available via our Salonology Gold Club. It's the main way that we help salon owners of all shapes and sizes to enjoy more freedom in their lives and more profit in their business.

I've made a special video, just for you readers of this book, to tell you more about it. If this book has got you excited in any way, then you won't want to miss this:

www.salonologygoldclub.com/book-bonus or scan the QR code.

Whether you'd like our guidance and experience to get this all set up in your business or whether you'd prefer to take the next steps alone, I'm grateful for you being here.

I hope your System helps some of your business dreams come true, just like it did for us.

To your success,

Ryan

Scan me for the bonus!

REFERENCES

[1] Strugar, M. (2023). *Small Business Statistics UK Edition [2023].* Retrieved from https://cybercrew.uk/blog/small-business-statistics-uk/

[2] Abraham, J. (n.d.). *The power Parthenon strategy of geometric business growth.* Retrieved from: https://www.abraham.com/topic/three-ways-to-grow-your-business/

[3] Wertz, J. (2018). Don't spend 5 times more attracting new customers, nurture the existing ones. *Forbes.* Retrieved from https://www.forbes.com/sites/jiawertz/2018/09/12/dont-spend-5-times-more-attracting-new-customers-nurture-the-existing-ones/

[4] Nadia (2002). *How many ads do we see a day?* Siteefy. Retrieved from https://siteefy.com/how-many-ads-do-we-see-a-day/

[5] Smith, T (1885). *Successful advertising.* s.l.: Thomas Smith Agency.

[6] Smith, T (1885). *Successful advertising.* s.l.: Thomas Smith Agency.

[7] Nosto (2019). *Stackla survey reveals disconnect between the content consumers want & what marketers deliver.* Retrieved from: https://www.nosto.com/blog/report-consumer-marketing-perspectives-on-content-in-the-digital-age/

[8] Smith, T (1885). *Successful advertising.* s.l.: Thomas Smith Agency.

[9] Burg, B. (n.d.). *All things being equal...* Retrieved from: https://burg.com/2010/04/all-things-being-equal/

[10] Paget, S. (2023). *Local consumer review survey 2023.* Retrieved from: https://www.brightlocal.com/research/local-consumer-review-survey/

[11] Abraham, J. (n.d.). *The power Parthenon strategy of geometric business growth.* Retrieved from: https://www.abraham.com/topic/three-ways-to-grow-your-business/

[12] Wertz, J. (2018). Don't spend 5 times more attracting new customers, nurture the existing ones. *Forbes.* Retrieved from https://www.forbes.com/sites/jiawertz/2018/09/12/dont-spend-5-times-more-attracting-new-customers-nurture-the-existing-ones/

[13] Marketing Charts (2019). *Online video consumption continues to rise globally.* Retrieved from: https://www.marketingcharts.com/digital/video-110520

[14] Stein, A. (2021). *Your cheat sheet to Google's 200 (known) ranking factors*. Hubspot. Retrieved from: https://blog.hubspot.com/marketing/google-ranking-algorithm-infographic

[15] Power Reviews (2018). *Growing reliance on reviews*. Retrieved from: https://www.powerreviews.com/wp-content/uploads/2018/03/The-Growing-Power-of-Reviews.pdf

[16] WhatsApp (2020). *New ways to connect with businesses on WhatsApp*. Meta. Retrieved from: https://about.fb.com/news/2020/07/connect-with-businesses-on-whatsapp/

ABOUT THE AUTHOR

Ryan Power is a beauty business success coach and speaker and also the author of the best-selling book *The Customer Is Always Right – And 7.5 Other Outdated Myths Which Are Destroying Your Beauty Salon Business.*

He and his wife Hollie owned their successful day spa and salon for over a decade before selling it to concentrate on their coaching brand, Salonology, through which they now help others to create their dream businesses.

They currently coach and mentor more than 450 salon owners as a part of their VIP Gold Club membership programme.

Ryan, Hollie and their dog Maverick reside by the sea in sunny Bournemouth, on the south coast of England.

To work with Ryan and Hollie,
visit **www.salonologygoldclub.com**